HOW TO MAKE LOVE
TO A MOVIE STAR

Writing for Film

The Exile Silver Screen Series

HOW TO MAKE LOVE
TO A MOVIE STAR

～ *Writing for Film* ～

Norman Snider

Library and Archives Canada Cataloguing in Publication

Snider, Norman, 1945-
    How to make love to a movie star : writing for film / Norman Snider.

(The Exile silver screen series)
ISBN 978-1-55096-245-1

    1. Motion picture authorship. 2. Television authorship. I. Title.
II. Series: Exile silver screen series.

PN1996.S63 2012   808.2'3   C2012-902157-1

Design and Composition by Hourglass Angels~mc
Typeset in Garamond at the Moons of Jupiter Studios
Photographs provided by Photofest
Printed by Imprimerie Gauvin

Published by Exile Editions Ltd ~ www.ExileEditions.com
144483 Southgate Road 14 – GD, Holstein, Ontario, N0G 2A0
Printed and Bound in Canada in 2012

The publisher would like to acknowledge the financial support of the Canada
Council for the Arts, the Government of Canada through the Canada Book
Fund (CBF), the Ontario Arts Council, and the Ontario Media Development
Corporation, for our publishing activities.

Canadian Sales: The Canadian Manda Group, 165 Dufferin Street,
Toronto ON M6K 3H6   www.mandagroup.com   416 516 0911

North American and international Distribution, and U.S. Sales:
Independent Publishers Group, 814 North Franklin Street,
Chicago IL 60610   www.ipgbook.com   toll free: 1 800 888 4741

Contents

Scan this QR with your smartphone/mobile device for a six-minute video
featuring Norman Snider talking about various aspects of the book.
Or, access the video at: www.tinyurl.com/AnIntroductionToScreenwriting

INTRODUCTION

by Norman Snider

A screenplay is a form of writing unlike any other. The novel, short story, poem, essay, newspaper or magazine article, and stage play all have their conventions and requirements, each unique to the demands of the particular medium. Whether written for the big screen of the movies or the small screen of television, a screenplay resembles a musical score. It is not a work of art in itself; it is a blueprint. That is, a screenplay has no real existence unless it is transformed into a film with actors and technicians, just as a symphony remains unheard unless an orchestra performs it in a hall or on a recording.

Movies and television drama are the most social of literary forms in that they exist only if they are shown or broadcast publicly. You cannot separate a film from an audience or, consequently, from its culture.

All the same, a screenplay is an intimate literary work: i.e., sentences composed of written words, on a page. Northrop Frye said it best that movies are part of an umbrella category called literature. The screenplay itself, however, is a bastard form, combining elements of the stage play, the novel, and journalism, even poetry. Nonetheless, it is a demanding, precise, highly organized mode hedged about with generally recognized conventions that the novice screenwriter ignores at his or her peril.

Movies, in the hierarchy of media, dominate in contemporary society. A recent British study ranks the movies, in terms of public interest, higher than sports, politics, and even restaurants. Attendance at movie theatres in the United States tops out at more than a billion a year. For better or worse, the feature film has largely replaced both the novel and stage play as the premier narrative and dramatic form of our culture. Celebrated movie directors now enjoy the social standing previously held by great novelists, as the screen in all its forms, from television to the laptop, comes to dominate modern society, replacing the printed page in the arena of consciousness.

Film has long since overtaken the stage as the premier dramatic medium. It was the poet Shelley who said that the vitality of drama was inseparable from the psychic health of a nation. He believed that the highest perfection of human society has always corresponded with the highest dramatic excellence, and that the extinction of the drama in a country marks the extinction of the energies that sustain the soul of social life. Shelley's remark can be confirmed by the tedium of any dinner party that neglects discussion of recent movies.

The prerequisite for writing movies is a passion for film. To write films, you must love them, and spend a lot of time plumbing their depths. And that's just the beginning. There are a thousand film scholars who comprehend the medium down to its bones but who could never write a film that would see the light of day.

All the same, the men and women you are likely to meet in the current world of the movies, including the stars themselves, are film buffs, with a detailed, even arcane knowledge and appreciation of film, and often possessed of expert knowledge of what makes a good screenplay. Long gone are the days of the baggy pants, cigar-smoking movie producer. Even if you aspire to write a humble horror film, you had better know the German expressionism of *The Cabinet of Dr. Caligari* and *Nosferatu*. The men and women execs you'll meet who have the power to turn your screenplay into a movie not so long ago were writing informed essays about them at film schools like Yale and UCLA, where the profs don't just pass the time of day watching movies on a Saturday afternoon.

It is a commonplace that film is a language, with its own grammar, its history of usage, its history of conjunctions – those ifs, ands, or buts that constitute an aesthetic. It is nonetheless shocking that so many aspiring screenwriters don't speak the language of the medium in which they desire to create.

The language of film is admittedly a difficult one to learn. Film comes at an audience at speed. Its power is derived in part from its existential immediacy. Although the DVD has improved matters somewhat, you still cannot read a movie at leisure like you do a page of prose. However, movie scripts are now widely available online in their printed form and as books. As such, they can be subject to the same sort of analysis or close reading as any poem or novel.

Strange to say, many novice screenwriters are reluctant to undertake a close analysis of even the most recent movies, the ones they claim most to admire. If they take the trouble to read and reread current screenplays in combination with the classics, they will discover that every teen comedy, every adolescent CGI (computer-generated imagery) superhero epic, every shallow family sitcom, obeys the same ancient rules and conventions of the form.

Beginning, middle, end.

Character, plot, dialogue.

Protagonist, antagonist.

Simple, huh?

How hard can it be?

A screenplay is 100 pages.

A couple pages a day.

Three months tops, you're ready to go skiing in Aspen with Tom and Katie.

Anybody could do it.

Yet, these simple Aristotelian categories are fathoms deep. The planet is teeming with writers floundering in the oceanic depths. The mysteries of character and plot can take decades to comprehend and absorb – then act upon.

Here we encounter still another paradox of movie writing. The form of on-stage drama is ancient yet the content of movies is up to the moment. Like newspapers, movies are best when they are closest to the street, right now, today. More than any other medium, movies have the power to not only depict fashion, manners, and morals, but also to create them.

Whole generations learn the contemporary forms of courtship and marriage, even household decor, from the movies.

Humphrey Bogart makes smoking cigarettes look tough and elegant. His fans are lighting up for decades after.

Peter Fonda and Dennis Hopper hit the road on motorcycles in that 1960s artifact, *Easy Rider*. Now, on weekends, the highways are black with part-time Wild Ones.

What the aspiring screenwriter must do is take an ancient form and connect it to a live wire.

Movies have much in common with magic and with dreams. Like magic and dreams, movies are creatures of night, experienced in darkness. To a naïve audience, movies are completely mystery and magic. They emerge from a faraway place named Hollywood; the unsophisticated believe that the actors are just doing what comes naturally, making up their lines as they go along. Even more sophisticated viewers persist in believing that celebrity actors are very like the characters they portray on screen and are bitterly let down when that so often proves not to be the case.

Although movies can be used for serious artistic purpose, more often than not they serve as a momentary escape. Like dreams, this escape takes two forms: daydream or nightmare. The audience can daydream that it can have successful romantic adventures like Matt Damon or it can shudder, at a safe distance, at the contrived threats of a horror film or the *Grand Guignol* violence of a *Texas Chainsaw Massacre*.

Mind you, such daydreams in dark rooms are not confined to low-rent escapist movies. *Midnight in Paris*, by Woody Allen, represents a common daydream of the literate; namely, going back into the "legendary" Paris of the 1920s, to live, if only for 90 minutes, in the story like stout-hearted Hemingway or fey, Gatsby-like Fitzgerald.

Whatever the case, the screenwriter must create a dramatic visual narrative that bears a closer relation to dreamscape than any docudrama or news report.

In this equation, the screenwriter holds an equivocal position. There have been many celebrity novelists, from Tolstoy to Hemingway to Faulkner to Atwood. There are very few celebrity screenwriters; wanting to be a screenwriter is like aspiring to the status of co-pilot. Co-pilots, however, can get rich. There is a screenwriter hierarchy going from the big-money guys, who can get $250,000 a week from the studios and millions for their scripts, down to the struggling indie scribes, who spend years writing and rewriting for the love of it, hoping against hope for a production.

Given these conditions, well-schooled literary writers often regard the rough-and-tumble of the movie business as an affront to their dignity, never mind the difficulty of the form itself. In the feature film, make no mistake, the screenwriter, whatever the force of his point of view, is merely a servant to the director's vision. While a screenplay is being written, frequently in collaboration with a director, all too often this vision is more accurately understood as a need to revise. So, the screenwriter had better comprehend that a screenplay in development is usually an idea in flux. And if further warning is needed, it is said of the director Francis Ford Coppola that he thinks a screenplay is like a newspaper, because he wants a new one every day. In this, he is not unique among directors or producers. Either through nervousness or boredom, they are unwilling to let a text settle.

So, any feature script is likely to go through as many as 20 revisions. Producers and directors believe that any screenplay, no matter how individual, can be rewritten by any other writer. In any one script idea, there are at least five very different movies to be found. In the process of bringing a film project to fruition, a process that can take many years, it's possible that a writer may write all five of these movies, each one of them very different in tone and approach. Several writers may be called upon to attempt one or several of the many revisions.

Despite these – often demeaning – difficulties, thousands of amateur and professional writers continue to attempt to write screenplays. Newspaper reporters, television producers, advertising copywriters, and other low toilers in the mass media, instead of dreaming of the novel they will write one day, as they once did, now daydream about the screenplay that will catapult them into the killer high life of champagne, mega-dollars, and actresses.

Yet, they should know, they should be warned that the transition from page to screen is not easy. The habits of a lifetime conspire against the contemporary writer, the literary novelist. The modern novelist, who has often spent a goodly portion of his career in academia, nourishing himself on the classics of high literature, often recoils at both the sheer vulgarity of what appears on movie screens and the creative ethos of the writing that puts it there. The conventions of literary modernism, long enshrined in Departments of Literature around the world, have codified the formal rebellions of Joyce, Woolf, Faulkner, et al. against the traditional representations of character and plot that are the bread and butter of movie storytelling.

Both the novel and film concern themselves with storytelling, yet film, as a whole, as a popular art and a mass medium, bears a much closer relation, not just to dream, but to the traditions of commercial fiction, even pulp fiction, in a route that can be traced via the comic book to the dime novels of the 19th century.

The Godfather, a classic of the cinema, is based on a pulp bestseller by Mario Puzo. *The Maltese Falcon* and *2001: A Space Odyssey* are, in their separate ways, masterpieces of cinema. The books on which they are based are both prime examples of commercial, genre fiction. Few classic novels make great movies. Except for films like Ken Russell's adaptation of D.H. Lawrence's *Women in Love*, movie classics are much more frequently drawn from commercial bestsellers: *Gone with the Wind*.

As a result, writers with a literary background don't take commercial cinema seriously. But, believe me, the $300 million or so a successful commercial movie can generate is taken very seriously by the people who make them. These movies cost money to produce; outside the studios, a lot of hard-to-raise money. Even the cheapest straight-to-DVD piece of schlock requires that somebody raise a couple of million dollars towards its production. Furthermore, movies and television are a mass media and, as such, they must satisfy the requirements of mass taste of the society from which they emerge. On odd occasions, these commercial products transcend that taste and attain the status of Art: Fellini emerged from the commercial Italian cinema, Truffaut from the French, Ingmar Bergman from the state-run movie industry of Sweden, Martin Scorsese from the Hollywood industry.

And so, for better or worse, film is a collaborative medium. If you don't play well with others, screenwriting is not for you. The employed screenwriter is anyone but a lone poet in his garret, anything but a romantic visionary. He is often a unionized, certainly highly paid professional who has more in common with actors than he does with academics, and more in common with the below-the-line technicians of film like cameramen and editors than he would like to admit.

The writing of screenplays is seldom fine writing, although it can be finely done by professionals. A beautiful prose style counts for less than nothing. I have read screenplays by prominent novelists that were beautifully and masterfully written but utterly unproduceable.

Nonetheless, at a preliminary stage, literary values need not be entirely absent from screenwriting because a script has to be actually read by those people who will not only provide the millions, but those celebrity actors whose participation will make it possible. Their interest and enthusiasm must be aroused – and this is an irony inimical to the industry – by the writer's art.

In fact, the industry term for the early version of the script meant for the delectation of the Suits is known as "the read." This draft contains writerly, literary, entirely superfluous pirouettes in prose meant to entice movie stars and amuse those jaded execs who have the power to green-light, as they say, a production. But once the film's a go, the screenplay's literary pirouettes are dispensed with as a distraction.

Neither is the novelist the only kind of scribe unsuited by temperament and habit to write for the movies.

Newsrooms are crammed with journalists, especially in the arts sections, who aspire to write screenplays. However, the first impulse of the journalist is to debunk, to expose, to capture that gotcha moment that skewers public figures, be they actors, politicians or sports celebrities.

Wrong for the movies.

In John Ford's classic western, *The Man Who Shot Liberty Valance,* James Stewart, playing an elderly prairie senator, attempts to explain to a reporter that his entire political career has been an imposture. The killing of the outlaw Liberty Valance, the act that turned the senator into a successful politician, was in fact committed by John Wayne. The reporter doesn't care.

"When the legend becomes fact," says Ford's reporter, "print the legend."

This is, as we shall see, the first duty of the screenwriter: to create larger-than-life characters, personae who can be inhabited by one of the reigning idols of the screen. The journalistic debunking impulse is completely antithetical to the spirit of the movies.

Every once in a while, a major director, such as Michael Mann, out of praiseworthy civic concern, will put out a movie like *The Insider*, starring Russell Crowe as a dour whistleblower exposing the misdeeds of the tobacco industry. But, it is no accident that *The Insider* trails all of Mann's other films in popularity. No, the film audience wants to see heartthrob Johnny Depp as John Dillinger, the legendary outlaw, in Mann's *Public Enemies* or glamorous Al Pacino and Robert De Niro as heroic cops and robbers in *Heat*.

Given this, the aspiring screen dramatist should ask himself: what makes a movie hero? By definition, a hero is a man or woman who, buffeted by the odds, conquers great difficulties. Real-life heroes are often celebrated for their great skill. But talent and achievement by themselves do not make movie heroes. Being an actual living legend is not good enough. For instance, there has never been a greater hockey player than Gordie Howe. Nobody is in a hurry to make a movie about his life. In the Aristotelian sense, nothing ever happened to him. And worse, all his life he was, from a dramatic point of view, almost entirely inarticulate. Not so, Gen. Douglas MacArthur, and for that matter, not so Moses. Old Testament admonitions aside, it is the job of the screenwriter not just to find but to create idols, false or otherwise.

In addition, the movies, since the silent era, have been concerned with creating sexual glamour. This aspect of film is somewhat better understood by advertising copywriters than journalists. It is the copywriter's job to glamorize homely items from beer to shaving cream. Screenwriters must create glamour and romance, sometimes out of very little. It's part of the job description. Like the directors who come from television commercials, they comprehend better than journalists how to glamorize a locale or a character by making both resemble a shiny advertisement as much as possible. However, going from a two-minute commercial to a two-hour feature film is not so easy either.

Gore Vidal, in his essays, often spoke of the Wise Hack, a grizzled old writer wreathed in cigar smoke, given to muttering sage advice from his table at the studio commissary. Movies have changed a great deal in their near century of existence, but whether writing for the silents or 3-D and CGI, the fundamentals, as retailed by the Wise Hack, have remained the same.

James M. Cain, a novelist and a screenwriter, in his *Paris Review* interview, recalled a real-life Wise Hack in the person of one Vincent Lawrence, a belly-up-to-the-bar screenwriter of the '30s who, usually uncredited, had worked, amongst dozens of others, on such films as *The Pride of the Yankees* and *Gunga Din*.

Lawrence spoke to Cain of "the one, the two, and the three" as his guiding principle in dramatic construction. When Cain allowed as to how Aristotle had said something similar, Lawrence said, "Who the hell is Aristotle and who did he ever lick?"

Nonetheless, the dynamic dialectic of the one, the two, and the three, or thesis, antithesis, and synthesis, is a useful principle to keep in mind in the construction of dramatic structure, scene and character.

Although Lawrence and the other hard-drinking Wise Hacks have long disappeared into the smog off Sunset Boulevard, their rough-and-ready instruction, handed down over the years, is still dispensed by veteran producers and literary agents, in much the same way ring lore is handed down in gyms, as well as by those sirens, the D-girls, as story development executives, largely women, are known. Their story wisdom, couched in a jargon easily ridiculed by the self-consciously literate, is a wisdom that is very useful, if you want to write movies.

Still, the fact is, savage absurdity rules the movie and television business. Taste is subjective. Suits can love a script on Monday and hate it by Tuesday; they all live in fear for their jobs. One bad call, yea or no, on a project can cost millions. Independent productions come with a ragbag of producers, each with their own, often uninformed, opinion. You're as good as your last script. It's hard to break in. Once in the biz, it's difficult to stay there.

Herewith: some practical advice, in the patois of the Wise Hack.

We live in a time of the primacy of the Star and the Celebrity, even in the age of High Concept, 3-D, IMAX, and CGI spectacle. Movie stars of all eras, including the present, have two main functions in the Industry. Number one, they "open" a picture. In the language of the fight game, they are a draw on a Friday night. Audiences go out, pay for parking and a babysitter, not to savor brilliant writing or direction but to see Brad Pitt or Nicole Kidman. Secondly, the leading actor "carries" a picture. In other words, the character he or she portrays must sustain audience interest throughout the length of the film. Otherwise, the audience is bored, twitches in its seat, changes the channel, and you, as a writer, along with the actors, director, producers and the investors who have put up their many millions, have failed.

In the culture of celebrity, the star actor or director reigns supreme. This is the prime message of the talent agents and producers to the writer: create a part a movie star wants to play.

Here we enter into dangerous territory – the psychology of an idol of the cinema.

Again, this is a subject where the novelist or journalist is at a disadvantage. For many, the culture of celebrity ranks amongst the prime excrescences of the age. Media historians can trace how the cult of celebrity is largely a product of technology and urbanization, how it rose in the late 19th century along with the telegraph and railways, how celebrities became role models, especially for adolescents, amidst the chaos and alienation of city life.

The screenwriting novice, arriving in Hollywood, by whatever stroke of good fortune, ready to look down on the intelligence of celebrities, will find that he is dealing with tough, shrewd people, advised by other tough, shrewd people, often in possession of a major chip on the shoulder as a result of the early rejection all actors and performers suffer in the early stages of their careers. The roles offered by producers in routine box-office fodder – romantic comedies, thrillers, family dramas – while lucrative, don't offer much in the way of prestige. Roles that are more unusual allow our movie star to give a showy performance, to demonstrate that he or she isn't merely a superficial creature of looks and charm but a true dramatic artist.

With the intensification of social alienation in the Internet Age, celebrities have attained the status of Virtual Friends, imaginary companions with whom much of the audience have closer psychic relations than they do with mere flesh and blood.

But who do they want to be on the screen?

What are they really like?

We will see, in the pages that follow, that motivation is the essence of cinematic character. Let us examine, for instance, the motivation of a major movie star. Money, continued fame, that's easy. But there is also prestige. The major studios may be offering our movie star roles that will earn him many millions, but not necessarily roles that will win an Oscar and other awards, allow him to appear in all his glory at film festivals from Venice to Cannes. Although literary writers find this hard to believe, a movie star celebrity is an artist, from Meryl Streep right down to the humble action hero. As an artist, he or she, just as much as any lyric poet, seeks creative satisfaction.

A few examples: Charlize Theron as a psycho lesbian killer in *Monster*, Colin Firth as a royal stutterer in *The King's Speech*, Sean Penn as the gay activist politician of San Francisco in *Milk* – Oscar winners all.

It is consequently the contention of this book that the creation of provocative character for high-wattage personalities, male or female, is the first order of business of the dramatist, be he veteran or neophyte. Create a grand, large-scale Shakespearian hero as your central character. This is not to say that you create a surefire Oscar-winning role first time out – merely an unusual role that a prominent performer thinks might lead to a stroll on the red carpet. It is also the contention of this book that all the other aspects of screenwriting spring from character. Plot, structure, theme, tone, action, and comedy – all the aspects of screenwriting springs from the creation of character.

The student writer often makes the mistake of contriving a plot into which he tries to insert character. We shall see that, of course, all these elements – character, plot, and theme – are indivisible, but in the end, writing for movies is about the creation of movie star roles. If your lead character doesn't fascinate, or fails to convince, your script will be lifeless and boring and will attract scant interest.

It is the primary business of the screenwriter to create this virtual transaction between the celebrity entertainer and the audience. Psychologists' research into dreams shows that star performers reach deep into the unconscious of the audience. Not only do star-struck teenagers daydream about celebrities, people of all ages are visited during sleep by these discarnate celebrity shades, so deep are they imbedded in the mass psyche. Through the process of identification, the screenwriter creates character, the vehicle the star travels to connect with the dreams of millions.

The two main principles of visual storytelling are so obvious they would seem not worth mentioning, yet most novice screenwriters apparently do not know them. The first is heard in every creative writing class from high school onwards. It is the first commandment of any form of storytelling.

Show, don't tell.

In other words, you are creating life as it happens in front of the audience's eyes: they need to see it. If they can't see it, it isn't a movie.

In the words of Vinny Lawrence, "If it ain't on the page, it ain't on the stage."

Second principle, courtesy George Bernard Shaw: "The essence of drama is conflict."

The simplest drama, down to a puppet show, is a dialogue. Few of us enjoy conflict in life, but the more conflict, the better in drama.

Conflict, i.e., drama, must permeate your screenplay at every level; it's what keeps an audience interested. Like a street fight just outside their front window, it will keep their attention.

And that is the first job of any artist: the creation of interest. The audience consists of millions of total strangers. You are faced by their indifference, if not outright hostility. You, as a writer, have to win them over, and then keep their attention for a couple hours.

That's the gig.

Now, an introductory word about process. There are several different ways about approaching the actual writing of a script. Like many aspects of the writing craft, it's subjective, a matter of habit and preference.

Many writers, bored with outlines, like to launch directly into a script without preparation. The fun, for them, consists in discovering their characters and theme. If they take a wrong turn, so be it. They're willing to jettison the pages and start again. Others write lengthy outlines, leaving no detail to chance. I've even heard of a writing team that videotapes its improvised scenes together, and then produces a transcript.

Networks and studios, however, structure their deals to demand an outline, a draft, two fixes and a polish. And you'll have to come up with a take to get the job in the first place.

In plain English: a fix is a rewrite, a take is a pitch or your briefest sketch of the story, usually delivered verbally. Execs don't like to read any more than they have to.

Usually, each stage involves many versions for the writer before he has a finished product he wishes to stake his reputation on. Once in a while, you hear of scripts written in a week of ecstatic composition. More often, they are the product of patient day-by-day labor.

In any event, it doesn't matter how the work is done, as long as it's good. No matter the genre, high or low, Duke Ellington's categorization of music holds true for writing as well: there are two types, good music and the other kind.

If he's going to be any good, the screenwriter has to believe that his form is of equal value to the novel, poem, or stage play. If he's going to be any good, he has to have the dedicated writer's sense of mission. A screenwriter's work must be personal, if it is going to be good; unlike a novelist's, it can never be solipsistic.

The same conventions apply to films whether they qualify as art or trash. *Citizen Kane* and *Chinatown* observe the same formal laws and conventions as *Rush Hour 3*.

The individual writer must find his own path and style inside these conventions. Originality consists in taking an angle of indirection, never meeting these conventions head-on. Flaunting the convention risks incoherence, while merely reproducing it turns the work stale. A top screenwriter, therefore, turns out to have an idiosyncratic point of view on character and life, usually because he has a complete understanding of the conventions. He knows the laws he's breaking and why.

Nobody can teach a beginning writer how to have such an idiosyncratic vision.

Either you have it or you don't. There is no course where you can learn it, no screenwriting expert who can teach it.

The best guide to developing a singular view I know is to believe your own eyes and ears and listen to what those interior voices are telling you; ignore all others.

If the writer can marry an idiosyncratic vision to the durable conventions of cinema, he or she will have mastered what is possibly the most powerful and persuasive art of our time.

CHARACTER

LIKE ANY OTHER FORM OF WRITING, screenwriting is intuitive. All of us have, in the course of a lifetime, seen a multitude of movies, and have absorbed their conventions, however unconsciously. Following the example of what he has absorbed from other films, if he has talent, the screenwriter *shows* us character by virtue of what he recalls from persons known in life. He can do this as simply and naturally as a painter renders a portrait, if he has the gift. Then, instruction is unnecessary.

However, if the student writer lacks a gift for characterization, method or craft is available to lend a helping hand. Craft enables the writer to break character down into its component parts and to build character from the ground up. This is not to say, however, that you can create character from a bunch of spare parts, like the Rabbi of Prague created the Golem, or Frankenstein created his Monster.

Character must be consistent throughout the course of a story. If a character is contradictory, he or she is said to wobble. Once a character wobbles, audience interest wobbles.

Or, as the Wise Hack would put it, the viewers are "out of the movie."

A writer creates a character by defining what the character does and what he says. This hasn't changed since the silents.

Dude comes out, pats the dog:

The good guy.

Dude comes out, kicks the dog:

The bad guy.

Usually, the people invented by a novice are dreary; they are the same, whether doctor, lawyer or Indian chief. They all talk in the identical idiom tonally – the writer talks to himself. As such, they fail to convince.

How then, does one create character?

A Hollywood veteran of the 1950s, one of those Wise Hacks, once told me he based every protagonist, be they cowboy, politico, or surgeon, on his mother, a *yiddishe* drama queen.

Whatever the dramatic situation, he asked himself, "What would my mother do?"

He knew his mom, rampant with inner conflicts, even in the guise of a gunslinger, would be of dramatic interest.

The lesson.

Look around and listen. Trust your eyes and ears.

Start taking notes.

IN THE WORLD OF MOVIES, there are many audiences. Know who you are writing for, who your audience is. Each has its preference as to character, especially protagonists. Cineplex audiences are likely to be between 15 and 30. They like CGI superheroes, nerd comedies, and action heroes. They also like family comedies and lovable animated creatures.

Cable audiences, on the other hand, are over 40, and they like dominant males and career women.

We all, no matter what our age, like certain types of people, known as stock characters; they automatically compel interest. Stock characters vary with the historical era. In classical drama, the Blind Seer and the Miser interested audiences. So did the Hapless Fool and the Swaggering Soldier.

Such stock characters have the virtue of being recognizable in a blink. The audience is able to greet them as old friends. But, watch out. Old friends, who have little or no depth, all too often end up as "cartoons." They grow stale.

Thankfully, stock characters, and the popularity of certain kinds of protagonists, change with the times. In an era when a tech tycoon like Steve Jobs or Bill Gates can be hailed as a supreme hero, its movies will necessarily celebrate the digital whiz, i.e., Mark Zuckerberg in *The Social Network*, Billy Beane and Peter Brand, the computer-ace sidekick played by Jonah Hill in *Moneyball*. These tech supermen, these keyboard jockeys, matter to the contemporary audience in the digital age just as much as John Wayne's soldier-heroes mattered to the WWII generation. Woody Allen, in his younger days, portrayed a character thrown up by the mass democratic education of the post-war era – a typically anxious and insecure member of the chattering classes – professor, writer, journalist, critic, teacher, intellectual – who wore his

3

angst like Linus wore his blanket in his comic search for meaning and a mate.

Every journeyman dramatist makes use of the characters of his who define the outline of his time. Original artists, however, capture personalities that have never been seen onscreen before. They define the new character types that society always presents. Or they give a stock character a new twist.

Zuckerberg, in *The Social Network,* as written by Aaron Sorkin, is the creepy epitome of the digital revolution: the tech genius as Asperger's victim.

Asperger's syndrome, a psychological malady, a mild form of autism, as David Mamet has pointed out, is prevalent among Ashkenazi Jews. Its prime characteristic, along with high intelligence, is extreme social ineptitude. The Asperger's type is so gripped by those brilliant notions going on in his own head he doesn't quite realize that other people are real and stumbles around socially as if he were wearing a blindfold. Fundamentally, the Asperger's victim is no wobbler: consistent to the end, he just doesn't listen.

You see who he is in the very first scene of *The Social Network*: where Zuckerberg is dumped by his college girlfriend, Erica.

Sorkin describes his character in terms of an animating paradox. Zuckerberg is 19 and "sweet-looking," but his lack of physically intimidating attributes "masks a very complicated anger."

Zuckerberg is a Harvard undergrad, obsessed with becoming a member of the elite social clubs found at that Ivy League university. A typical exchange between Mark and Erica reveals that even when he's talking to his girlfriend, skipping around from topic to topic, he's really talking to himself. "Since the beginning of the conversation about finals clubs," she says, " I may have had a birthday."

Burn After Reading, by the Coen Brothers, also depends, like *Social Network,* for its characterizations on close observation of typical personalities of the present era.

In this multi-character comic heist film, Brad Pitt plays personal trainer Chad Feldheimer, a man obsessed with physical fitness. Frances McDormand is Linda Litzke, similarly obsessed, but with cosmetic surgery. Harry Pfarrer, played by George Clooney, is also obsessed – but with do-it-yourself home renovation.

Like Sorkin, with his depiction of Zuckerberg, the Coen Brothers focused on these character's contemporary traits for the first time. The audience received that shock of recognition when it saw them on the screen. Of course, viewers may not be flattered by such satirical depictions, thus accounting for the very mixed reception of the film, since all the characters in the film are creatures of bad faith. The Coen Brothers had created, in a dark update of the Viennese playwright Arthur Schnitzler's *La Ronde,* a story, a plotline, wherein most of the characters were linked bodily, by sexual betrayal.

As we can see in Sorkin's description of Zuckerberg, the character's introduction is brief. The untested screenwriter tends to write paragraphs of character description to no purpose. In screenwriting, brevity is not just the soul of wit, but the soul of description as well.

For starters, physical appearance is the least important attribute you can describe when introducing a character. Age and one defining attribute is all that's necessary.

Cameron Crowe, in *Almost Famous,* introduces his young protagonist, William Miller, as "in his pre-teens" and "pale." His mother, Elaine, is 35; "tall" and "consumed by the fevered conversation" she's having with William. That's it. Everything else is defined by what they do and say in the course of the screenplay.

As with T.S. Eliot, the dramatist must search for an "objective correlative," the image that captures symbolically, that conveys symbolically, that conveys emotional qualities particular to a specific character directly to the audience. "Pale," in Cameron Crowe's physical description of his protagonist, is a visual representation of sensitivity. "Tall," indicates nobility. "Consumed by the fevered conversation" denotes a passionate nature. That is to say, physical description is not random; it symbolizes emotional characteristics in much the same way medieval drama personified Vice, Virtue, and Luxury as individuals.

So, a character's emotional and dramatic characteristics, for the purposes of visual storytelling, must be reflected in their appearance. An action hero should have wide shoulders, an athletic gait; he can't look like bespectacled Woody Allen. And so, too, a comic hero must have a humorous appearance. From Fatty Arbuckle to Jonah Hill, plumpness has been effectively seen as comical.

Even more important than appearance, for the purposes of drama, is the creation of temperament, and occupation.

Consider the following character description of Mary Sue, the chubby girlfriend of the bad guy, Brad, in *At Close Range*, by Nicholas Kazan. Mary Sue, Kazan tells us, "has the weirdly seductive manner of a cheap slut." Yet, Mary Sue, behind her trashy exterior, just may be brilliantly shrewd; it's difficult to

6

tell. "Chubby," as visual notation, is shorthand, perhaps comic, for blue collar. "The weirdly seductive manner of a cheap slut" is a quick and nasty bit of insight. As any reader of *Of Human Bondage* can attest, cheap sluts have a definite appeal to a male audience.

Next, a dash of mystery.

Is this cheap slut a dimwit, or deceptively shrewd? An audience will want to keep on watching in order to find out just which one she happens to be. Interest has been created. Remember: the essence of drama is conflict: a dramatic character is one who has this conflict embedded in his or her personality – the deeper the embedding, the less cartoonish the character. Mary Sue is a cheap slut who may be very elegantly shrewd. These inner qualities, as the conflict is revealed, create drama and thus interest in Mary Sue's character.

Actors want to play fascinating people. Fascinating characters are a combination of strength and weakness.

Because an audience craves characters with equal parts of light and shade in order to be fascinated, we see endless detectives on television with bad marriages, divorces, drinking problems, difficulties with their superiors, etc.

Without these darker characteristics, this inner drama, a detective, in his quest to bring crooks to justice, is a mere Dudley Do-Right and a bore. However, a strong writer is himself bored with clichéd character weaknesses and seeks out human flaws the viewers haven't seen before.

The writer and director Tony Gilroy, for instance, in *Michael Clayton,* gives the title character, portrayed by George Clooney, a gambling habit. A corporate lawyer with a gambling habit is not a character the viewer has seen too often, so he's interested, and keeps watching.

Conversely, an anti-hero, such as Robert De Niro's Jake LaMotta, in *Raging Bull*, must be given redeeming qualities in order to fascinate the audience.

LaMotta has been justly characterized as a "cockroach." LaMotta is an evil son-of-a-bitch, bursting with animal rage. He is both a masochist and sadist, beats his wife and his brother, and is possessed by uncontrollable appetites, which eventually cost him his career and his freedom.

Yet, on the positive side of the ledger, Jake is a talented fighter and a brave man, a champion unjustly deprived of his title by the mob corruption that is endemic to boxing; so we in the audience are content to watch this character battle his inner demons. If he were just a cockroach, we wouldn't want to spend ten minutes, let alone two hours of screen time, in his presence.

AUDIENCES CHANGE. MORE LIKELY, a character like LaMotta, without his redeeming virtues, is a good bet nowadays to serve as a bad guy or antagonist. The anti-hero was an audience favorite from the mid-'50s up until at least the '80s. But, in the midst of the Reagan/Thatcher revolution, the audience tired of him and reverted to its preference for more blandly traditional, likeable good guys.

Tom Cruise, for example, in his early career, from *Top Gun* on, portrayed one exemplary character: the hot shot who learns to be a team player. Tom Hanks, as in *Saving Private Ryan*, was often the likeable average man who rose to heroism. As Forrest Gump, he was a somewhat less than average man who managed to be present at the peak historical events of his time.

When considering a character, whether it's LaMotta or Gump, it's important to remember that the mood of the audience is in continual flux, not just decade-to-decade and year-to-year but also week-to-week. Don't bring out, as I once did, a horror movie in the same week a real-life serial killer like Jeffrey Dahmer has hit the front pages. The audience, confronted by real-life awfulness, is never in the mood for the Hollywood variety.

Identification is the psychological instrument by which you lead an audience to lose itself in the dream you are creating.

Who does a guy in the audience want to see up there on the screen?

Answer: *himself.*

And it follows that he doesn't want to see himself as Jeffrey Dahmer.

MOVIES ARE A MASS MEDIUM; the more people you can get to identify with your lead character, the more successful your story will be. Hence, find the lowest common emotional denominator – the character trait that is common to those viewers likely to see your film.

Here, writers encounter the single most important element of characterization: motivation. The word itself, unfortunately, has something comic about it. How many satirical skits exist where a method actor wanders about asking about his "motivation?"

Nonetheless, what the protagonist *wants,* even if it's just a ham sandwich, is the engine that propels him through the story. It is the antagonist's job to stop the guy from getting that sandwich. The resulting clash of wills, especially if the two "wills" are also in conflict within the protagonist's character, is what creates drama. The more elemental your hero's motivation, the more likely the audience is to share it, and the more likely they are to watch to the end of your film. After all, the most powerful motivation is primal. The desire to survive or to find a mate or have a child is elemental, fundamental to the human experience.

James Bond, as created by Ian Fleming, has the same primal motivation as the hero of many Mexican movies: Bond wants to kill all his enemies and make love to all the women. Nonetheless, even a character as successful with audiences as Bond has had to change with the times. In this age of family values, womanizers are no longer popular. Bond, in his latest incarnations, is a one-woman kind of guy.

If the audience disapproves of what your protagonist wants, they won't like your movie. They'll change the channel, or walk out.

IF MOTIVATION PROVIDES THE emotional force that drives your protagonist through the story, occupation and their attendant skills determine the context in which he or she will operate, as well as the genre of film you're writing. If your hero is a bank robber, you're dealing with the world of crime in the genre of the heist film. If your hero is a nightclub singer, you're writing a musical in the world of showbiz. But, whatever his nominal occupation, more than anything else, the typical protagonist, circa 2012, regardless of genre, must first of all be depicted as a Good Father and a Nice Guy. Whatever his skills or the context in which he operates, his attitude towards affable parenthood trumps everything else.

In *Knocked Up,* for example, Seth Rogen comes of age by abandoning the teen world of marijuana bongs and video games and learning the responsibilities of fatherhood. In *Drive,* the getaway driver played by Ryan Gosling, a surrogate dad like Alan Ladd in *Shane,* puts it all on the line for a single mom and her son. Denzel Washington, in *Man on Fire,* plays an almost identical role, except that he is a father surrogate, a young girl's bodyguard in kidnap-prone Mexico City. Today, in any event, fatherhood must enter into the equation.

Conversely, a lost soul, such as the one depicted by Ben Stiller in *Greenberg,* is defined by his lack of wife and kids. Roger Greenberg, with his compulsive letter writing, is a shallower, updated version of Saul Bellow's Moses Herzog. A 40-year-old dropout, he is mired in perennial adolescence. As the ladies-with-brassy-laughs are fond of saying, "He can't commit." So, he goes through life trying to reconnect with the important figures of his early 20s, when he played in a near-miss college rock outfit. In the 20 years since, his college friends have all but forgotten him. Now, a gloomy failure, he is a Mark Zuckerberg lacking the technological genius, a Woody Allen without the wit – not particularly pleasant to boot. And is, therefore, a modern-day figure of pathos.

This cinematic fixation on amiable family life applies to women protagonists too. Mavis Gary, portrayed by Charlize Theron, the attractive but alcoholic, bitchy protagonist of Diablo Cody's *Young Adult,* like Roger Greenberg, is unable to achieve parenthood. Like him, she presents another case of arrested development. Emotionally, she's never left high school. Achieving the status of mean-girl prom queen of a small town

Minnesota high school is the top moment of her life. Now, unmarried, she lives unhappily in the big city of Minneapolis, writing young adult fiction. When she returns to her small town, Gary's story shows, yet one more time, that, like Thomas Wolfe, You Can't Go Home Again.

Mavis Gary's goal is one which the audience should dislike: she wants to pluck Buddy, her high-school boyfriend, a new father who adores his wife, out of his marriage and drag him back to Minneapolis.

Yet, as bitchy and misguided as Mavis is, we sympathize with her predicament. She wants to be married and have a family, as does Roger Greenberg.

The mistakes these characters make in achieving those goals render them all too human, so the audience is willing to stay with their story, since they approve of their goals.

The inner conflict between their desires and the character flaws of narcissism and extended adolescence that prevent both Mavis and Roger from satisfying them is what creates the drama that keeps the viewers watching their stories.

In a sense, the characters share with the audience that they too are the victims of a youth culture that encourages perennial childhood. Yet, both these movies suggest that their protagonists remain unmarried... *because they are not nice.*

It is the rare film, such as *Greenberg* or *Young Adult,* which has the courage to introduce an even slightly unlikable protagonist. Both movies fail to give their hero a redemptory child, although *Greenberg* does give its protagonist a dog to be kind to. (Theron does have a cute dog, but she neglects it.)

Perhaps the bravest film ever to feature an unlikable protagonist is Scorsese's *The King of Comedy*. Robert De Niro's Rupert Pupkin, an autograph hound and failed comic who lives with his mother, takes a talk-show host hostage, in order to get on television. Pupkin doesn't have a pet, he isn't nice to children, he learns no redemptive lessons, and he's as nasty at the end of the movie as he is in the beginning.

Yet, the audience approves of his goal as well: Pupkin wants to be famous. As long as the audience approves of your character's goal, you can give him or her every possible negative personality trait and get away with it.

Oddly enough, for the writer, a disagreeable character like Mavis Gary or Rupert Pupkin may just do the trick in attracting a star performer. Star actors like De Niro or Theron crave an acting challenge. And making an almost completely unlikable character palatable to the viewer is certainly that and more.

Whether the central character is likeable or not, no theme, even fatherhood, is in itself dishonest. In *Biutiful,* Javier Bardem is a Good Father, but one treated entirely without sentimentality. His Barcelona street hustler has an alcoholic, promiscuous, bi-polar ex-wife, a bedwetting son, the cops on his butt, and terminal cancer.

As depicted by the Mexican director, Alejandro González Innaritu, the Bardem character, Uxbal, is a towering study in nobility, as he struggles against a host of afflictions. Uxbal weeps, rages, laughs, loves, dreams, and dies. The aspiring writer can do no better than to study this show-stopping role. It's the sort of part lead actors adore. It won Bardem several Best Actor awards.

FRITZ LANG, IN HIS MEMOIRS, recounts how the most important thing he had to learn when he came to Hollywood from Germany in the 1930s was the nature of the American film protagonist. In Germany, the hero was always a superman; in Hollywood, just an average guy.

Things have changed very little since Lang's day. It's a time when billionaire tycoons like Mark Zuckerberg shuffle around in jeans and sneakers. In American society as such, Cinderella is a theme that seldom fails. Whether the hero is a rocker or a socker makes small difference to the essentials of the character's motivation. The American hero, as exemplified by Tom Cruise or Tom Hanks, who would have been a superman in the Berlin of the 1930s, affects to be just an average guy who wants to… *make it to the top.*

Once you've settled on what the protagonist desires, you can turn your attention to other issues. If your protagonist is a funny person to whom funny things happen, it's a strong bet you'll be writing a comedy.

If you're writing a romantic comedy, your protagonist ought to be an attractive person in their 20s. If they're a senior, you're writing *On Golden Pond*, about love in old age and its particular problems.

ONCE MOTIVATION AND OCCUPATION are established, other, less important character traits can be added. These are the character's ethnic, social, and educational background. Is your character Jamaican or WASP? From a middle-class Toronto family in Leaside or from upper-class Rosedale?

Aside from description of physical appearance, these matters can be defined in a couple lines of dialogue. In *Pretty*

Woman, Julia Roberts asks Richard Gere, "How far did you go in school?" He answers: "I went all the way."

The audience now knows all they need about Gere's background.

ONCE THE WRITER HAS SETTLED on motivation, the key to creating further persuasive character trait is to determine spoken idiom. Defining manners of speech, pet phrases, sentence order and intonation all serve to depict ethnic and social background, as well as occupation.

Every occupation has its characteristic jargon. Every ethnic group has its characteristic idiom. Take, for example, the rogue LAPD narc portrayed by Denzel Washington in *Training Day,* written by David Ayer. His idiom is a compendium of California cop *patois.* For instance, a police night shift is a "mid-watch." "Homeboy did three years in the *Boyna Roja,*" means the Latino dude spent some time as a Red Beret commando in El Salvador. A training officer is a "T.O." A narcotic detective's unmarked vehicle is a "G-ride." He even has a pet phrase: "My nigga."

These are the idiomatic details that help define a character and make him persuasive. Ayer has clearly gone to a lot of trouble to spend time in patrol cars amongst homeboy L.A. cops and listened to how they speak. The aspiring screenwriter, if he wants to write a convincing detective, should do the research, somehow meet a narc, and learn the authentic idiom of his gritty occupation. Otherwise, he'll merely be aping other detective characters in other movies.

It's important to know that every ethnic group has a characteristic way of bending the English language to the ways of its native tongue. The aspiring screenwriter must study them all with the enthusiasm of an ethno-anthropologist.

For instance, Liam Neeson, playing the 18-century Scots outlaw and folk hero Rob Roy in Alan Sharp's script. Rob Roy McGregor threatens a cattle thief thus: "Are you not better dead this morning after a good hump and a belly full of beef?" The antique usage is conveyed by the formality of *"Are you not?"* The fact that Rob Roy is originally a Gaelic speaker is conveyed by the inverted sentence order, *"Are you not better dead this morning?"* I defy any actor to say that line of dialogue and not speak with a Celtic lilt.

Whole careers, let alone a single character, can be defined by a memorable pet phrase. An obvious example: *The Godfather's*, "I'm gonna make him an offer he won't refuse."

All these elements of character – occupational jargon, ethnic idiom and pet phrases – need to be accomplished with a light touch. When it comes to ethnic idiom, a little bit goes a long way.

I was once developing a script with Bob Rafelson, the notorious badass director of *Five Easy Pieces*. (Rafelson had cold-cocked a studio exec with an ashtray; earning himself five years of Hollywood unemployment for his pains.) One of our characters was an Italian porno king. I gave this mob guy plenty of Mulberry Street in his dialogue.

Rafelson's response:

"Too much marinara sauce."

Which tells you much of what you need to know about Bob Rafelson.

If you're not careful, a dreaded stereotype – the stage Irishman, black dude, or ruthless Italian gangster – will sink your script. You will have succeeded only in creating not a living character, but a flimsy persona manufactured out of pure cardboard, that is, past performances.

Once you've decided on a character's verbal idiom, you can move onto his idiom of action, his habitual style of behavior. David Ayer's rogue cop in *Training Day* is based on the corrupt narcotics detectives exposed in the Rampart scandal in Los Angeles in the late 1990s. The Rampart cops' party tricks included unprovoked shootings, beatings, planting of evidence, theft and dealing of narcotics, framing of suspects and perjury.

In the bygone days of *Raging Bull*, Detective Alonzo Harris would likely have been the anti-hero protagonist of the film. Twenty years later, he plays the antagonist to the stock all-American father hero, Jake Hoyt, played by Ethan Hawke.

Alonzo is Jake's treacherous boss. As a character, he is precisely observed: Alonzo is king of the jungle in the multicultural inner city. Ayer even provides Alonzo with a philosophy of love and marriage. Looking over some beautiful Latinas on the street, he mocks Jake's wife as a "Nordic cheerleader" and tells him that "the brown woman is the fine woman." And he advises Jake to give her ten more babies to push around.

Alonzo Harris is neither particularly likeable nor, with his multiple mistresses and their many children, likely to win any father-of-the-year awards. In this case, Jake Hoyt, the young cop, serves as what is known as "the point-of-view character." In other words, he functions as the audience's window on Denzel Washington's bad lieutenant, who is the real focal point of interest of the story. The audience turns out to see the movie star Denzel Washington play a magnificently evil bad guy. The point-of-view character is a kind of storytelling prophylactic. He allows us to enjoy the evil doings of the bad cop without our being forced to root for him.

Nick Carraway, in *The Great Gatsby*, is the greatest point-of-view character in all literature. The hero of Fitzgerald's story is Jay Gatsby. But Fitzgerald, the star of the *Saturday Evening Post*, and well-versed in the ways of commercial storytelling, knew better than to present a bootlegger, no matter how unlikely, front and center. So he told his story through Nick Carraway.

The point-of-view character is the narrative equivalent of safe sex. Nonetheless, he has his virtues. The point-of-view character allows the writer to present the antagonist in his full villainous glory. With an anti-hero protagonist, much energy must be spent giving the character a "sympathetic" side. The audience resists spending two hours looking at the world through the eyes of a complete villain. Whether Jack Abramoff or J. Edgar Hoover, the writer is compelled to trot out children and dogs and aged parents for the guy to pat, just to show he's not completely beyond redemption.

Gordon Gekko, in *Wall Street*, however, is another personage thought so uniformly reprehensible that he can only be seen through the filter of a point-of-view protagonist. Bud Fox, the naïve young trader, serves as a foil for Gekko in his magnificent, leveraged-buyout-hustling villainy. *Wall Street*, however, is not about Fox. The antagonist is the memorable character and the star role.

Even Henry Hill, in Scorsese's uncompromising *Goodfellas*, is something of a point-of-view character, although he's a mob guy himself. The Hill character is frequently scandalized at the brutality and violence of Joe Pesci's Tommy DeVito.

In *Training Day,* playing Jake Hoyt for a fall guy in his corrupt schemes, Alonzo forces him to smoke PCP-laced marijuana at gunpoint, implicates him in a drug rip-off, has him shot and then, when this doesn't work, sets him up to be murdered by Salvadoran gangbangers.

Every one of these evil actions represents Det. Alonzo Harris' idiom of behavior as a corrupt cop. If David Ayer were to make him do something generous and whimsical, his character would wobble.

He would be acting *out of character.*

But consistency in the invention of character must never become predictability. The best characters, like De Niro in *Taxi Driver* or *Mean Streets,* are also the most dangerous and unpredictable.

A writer, who intentionally makes one of his people act out of character, does not set them wobbling but rather makes them unpredictable.

Elmore Leonard, for example, in his novels and the films and television series made from his books, uses this idiosyncratic switch move: two bad guys who have been on a collision course, instead of having it out, join forces in order to rip off a third party. Or, conversely: a character he has set up as the hero's buddy and helpmate is suddenly, and usually violently, revealed as on the side of the antagonist. Essentially, it's a change in the nature of the character: from nasty to nice, or vice versa.

LET US NOW CONSIDER A CHARACTER much more innocent than Alonzo Harris, Gordon Gekko, or Henry Hill.

Juno MacGuff.

A Good Mother.

The creation of this character, by Diablo Cody, is a minor masterpiece of successful audience manipulation. Like *Knocked Up,* the movie is about an unplanned pregnancy. Juno is a liberated teenager, a weird kid who digs punk rock and horror movies and who gets pregnant.

But, get this, it's sweet: *she's anti-abortion.*

Juno's a hip chick, but her four-square morality puts her at odds with the pro-choice abortion culture, which Cody characterizes as dopey and gauche and prone to boysenberry-favored condoms.

Unlike Alonzo Harris, who is a product of on-the-scene research, Juno MacGuff is a classic example of Hollywood fabrication of character, which conflates sheer fantasy with authentic detail.

Juno talks in a bubblegum-teen dialect all of her own devising. Unlike the authentic narco jargon devised by Ayer, Diablo Cody seems to have invented Juno's *patois,* a combo of slang and the precociously witty, out of nothing. "Hi, " she says, "I'm calling to procure a hasty abortion." Or, she claims, kittenishly, that in China they give away babies like free IPods at sporting events.

Juno's idiom of action is also completely in character. Unable to contemplate abortion, she pluckily locates a childless couple that wants to adopt. The husband is a frustrated rocker who is mad about horror movies. Plucky in romance as well, she badgers her hapless passive boyfriend to "commit."

Punk-rock oddball Juno MacGuff may be, but all her motivation, her every action is calculated to win the Tea Party Good Housekeeping Seal of Approval.

Det. Alonzo Harris is drawn from life; Juno MacGuff is a fantasy. They each represent a different approach to the creation of character. Each works on its own terms. Yet, "Juno MacGuff" is a manipulative Tinseltown fabrication; "Alonzo Harris" has the ring of truth.

In the creation of these characters, writers combine authentic realism and utter fantasy in odd ways. Consider, for instance, the character of the private dick as portrayed by Humphrey Bogart, the most popular screen actor of all time, in his signature *noir* roles: Sam Spade in *The Maltese Falcon* and Philip Marlowe in *The Big Sleep*.

Dashiell Hammett, who created the Spade character, had worked as a Pinkerton operative after service in WWI. Unlike, Agatha Christie, say, he knew a great deal about the world of crime and police. Yet, Hammett recalled in an interview that he had based the Spade character on the fantasies that the detectives he knew had about themselves. In his own way, Sam Spade is as much a fabrication as Juno MacGuff.

Hammett's creation, Sam Spade, is a hard, shifty dude who comes out on top of every confrontation: pretty much a superman. Yet, almost every one of these confrontations given us by the writer is verbal; the movie is very like a stage play, consisting mostly of witty dialogue set in interiors. Because he is so eloquent, so much not the strong, silent type, Bogart appeals to the identical urban audience as Woody Allen for whom words are as important as actions. It's no accident that Hammett spent the latter part of his writing career helping out Lillian Hellman with her highly literate Broadway stage plays.

In a way, the private dick is a metaphor for the writer himself, especially in the case of Raymond Chandler's Philip Marlowe, who is himself as much fantasy as Spade. Marlowe is observant like the writer, articulate. He represents an individual point of view opposed to the collective wisdom of his society.

The one antagonist Hammett has Bogart subdue physically is Wilmer, the gunsel. (The word, derived from the Yiddish *gendzel,* "gosling," means passive homosexual, not gunman. Or, one who is goosed. Or, "on the gooseberry lay." A bit of 1920s prison slang sly Hammett slipped by the censors.)

But then, Bogart's "dick" is well named. The dick represents the missing male principle: Sydney Greenstreet, Peter Lorre, Elisha Cook, Jr., the *femme fatale,* Brigid O'Shaughnessy, are all women or gay.

The dick beats them all.

However, Hammett renders the milieu in which the private dick achieves this daydream of conquest with scrupulous realism. As Hammett writes him, Spade is cautious and prudent. He never makes a move without consulting a criminal lawyer who he keeps on retainer. Hammett gives Spade a network of contacts among both the cops and the crooks; he is well connected in all the municipal institutions of San Francisco.

Hammett also supplies Spade with an antique knightly code.

'When a man's partner is killed, he's supposed to do something about it. It doesn't make any difference what you thought of him. He was your partner and you're supposed to do something about it."

In *The Big Sleep*, the Bogart character, this time invented by Raymond Chandler, is even more familiarly the knight errant. Where Hammett's detective is almost half crook, Philip

Marlowe is self-consciously incorruptible. Chandler himself was obsessed with his status as an English gentleman forced to live beneath his status in the American democratic Inferno.

Thus the credo of Philip Marlowe:

"Down these means streets, a man must go who is not himself mean, who is neither tarnished nor afraid...

At the behest of an impotent old man, General Sternwood, the Bogart character created by Chandler must bring to heel a pair of errant daughters, much given, it is said, to slick men, drugs, and long-shot bets. Once again, in Marlowe, Chandler creates the missing male principle.

Marlowe behaves with much more gallantry than the frankly underhanded Spade. But then, Chandler knew far less of the authentic world of crime than did Hammett. But Chandler improved the Bogart character, for dramatic purposes at least, by making him much more of a loser. Sitting in his seedy office, without clients, Marlowe is more the underdog than Spade. Having positioned him near the bottom of society, there is more drama for Chandler to exploit in his character's opposition to the rich, decadent world represented by General Sternwood and his daughters. Marlowe is also more sentimental. He gets cozy with Lauren Bacall's heiress where Sam Spade eventually hangs the rap on Brigid O'Shaughnessy.

"Yes, angel, I'm gonna send you over."

After Spade and Marlowe, the cinematic private dicks appeared in great profusion in the 1950s and 1960s, from Mike Hammer to Lew Archer down to a dozen lesser lights. They all had world-weary attitudes, battered fedoras and bottles of whisky in the desk drawer of their down-at-heels offices.

When, in 1974, Robert Towne came to create Jake Gittes, Jack Nicholson's detective character in the neo-*noir Chinatown*, directed by Roman Polanski, he was updating what had by then become a thoroughly stale character. Towne remade the character by adding concepts taken from high culture to the pop figure of the private eye, combined with the authentic details of Los Angeles' social history.

Gittes is a direct descendant of the Bogart character. The writer, Towne, reprises several of the themes of *The Big Sleep* with Faye Dunaway updating Lauren Bacall as the wandering daughter. Yet, *Chinatown* is *noir* informed by Freud and dark European romanticism. Like Marlowe, Gittes is a metaphor for the writer, but, unlike Marlowe, he is a tormented soul himself, haunted by the past. With the corrupt exploitative Los Angeles tycoon, Noah Cross, as the dick's antagonist, and incest on the horizon, the Oedipal theme is paramount. Towne elevates Hammett's pulp-detective character with tropes taken from Marx and Freud.

Although set in the 1937, *Chinatown* is very much an artifact of its year of production, 1974, and so is Nicholson's Gittes, who is just as well connected as Spade – he has good friends at the newspapers, at the morgue, and at the LAPD. Specializing in matrimonial disputes, Gittes has done well for himself, even if Towne makes him a little ashamed of what he does for a living. He's the prosperous boss of a large detective agency.

But there's a big difference between the characters created by Hammett and Towne. Although his dramatic confrontations – except for a bout with a diminutive thug with a knife, played by Polanski – like Spade's, are mostly verbal, Gittes loses most of them; he is anything but a superman. Like Robert Altman's update of Marlowe himself in *The Long Goodbye*, Towne's downbeat character is baffled by the mystery in which he is enmeshed. Gittes, despite his sharp suits and two-tone oxfords, is very much a man of the counterculture, yet another victim of the System. A tarnished knight errant, his investigation results in tragedy – the murder of Faye Dunaway at the hands of the satanic father, Noah Cross, who is played by the director of *The Maltese Falcon,* John Huston.

Cross, a predatory champion of frontier-style business enterprise, once owned the city's water supply. He is also despoiling the moral environment. He has raped both his daughter and the Owens Valley. He also owns the cops. As the literary critic George Steiner points out, the theme of incest, with its defiance of social conventions and its pursuit of rare and prohibited experience, haunts the romantic imagination.

"Forget it, Jake. It's Chinatown."

Or maybe just Hollywood.

Based on the California Water Wars of the 1910s and 1920s, *Chinatown,* Towne's screenplay, probably comes closest to Jean-Luc Godard's definition of cinema: truth, 24 frames a second.

Nonetheless, the private dick created by Hammett and then by Towne is no longer a viable character for the present-day audience. The complicated business, political and erotic puzzle that baffles Gittes just bores today's audience; his defeat at the hands of a corrupt system merely demoralizes them. Today's family audience doesn't have the nerves for tragedy. It dislikes films without happy endings.

So, the character of the detective goes through another sea change as we come up to the present time. By contrast to Gittes, let's explore the character of the detective as presently envisaged in Guy Ritchie update of Arthur Conan Doyle's classic creation, *Sherlock Holmes*, as portrayed by Robert Downey, Jr. Conan Doyle's original character was an eccentric cerebral genius of deduction. As reinvented by Richie and his writers, he is all brawn: a literal superman; the detective as bodybuilding superhero. The London in which he lives is a kind of sci-fi computer-generated fantasy city.

Unlike the cadaverous original, Downey's Holmes is a splendid physical specimen, equipped with Bruce Lee-style martial arts skills, who prevails, stripped to the waist, against all comers in underground boxing matches. Unlike the traditional detective, the new, Schwarzenegger-ized Holmes is a spectacular action hero. His deductive super powers are more like telepathy than logical reasoning. His relationship with Dr. Watson is a bromance. The good doctor, in the original, was definitely a being of a lesser order, a plodding *bourgeois* to Holmes' aristocratic detective, a sidekick. Now, he's more like Holmes' high-school buddy, an equal. All the same, Ritchie knew what he was doing and his film was a success.

Ritchie's Sherlock Holmes resembles Batman more than Sam Spade. If Hammett's character represented an adult fantasy of virility, the Sherlock Holmes character update, like that of Juno MacGuff, is another adolescent daydream, as befitting the cartoonish requirements of the teenage audience for which it is meant.

Even more than the updated Holmes, the pre-eminent contemporary fantasy detective is Lisbeth Salander the outlaw computer hacker protagonist of *The Girl with the Dragon Tattoo*.

If Sam Spade represents the knight errant gone missing, Lisbeth is the avenging angel of man-hating retribution. Her character, part abandoned child, part computer genius, inhabits the dramatic paradox that makes a pop culture persona fascinating. If Spade's beat is crime in the city, Lisbeth's is malfeasance within the family. (Chandler famously said that Hammett took murder out of the Venetian vase and dropped it in the alley. With Stieg Larsson, we're back in the vase.)

Like Mark Zuckerberg in *The Social Network*, Lisbeth Salander is an adolescent who confronts the adult world and triumphs, thus allowing both adult and teenage viewers to identify with the character. Like Zuckerberg, she is a computer ace, another keyboard jockey. (This aspect of her character is the least persuasive. Lisbeth's computer skills, as presented in the movie, seem limited to looking things up on Google.) Her sidekick, Daniel Craig, who also plays James Bond, plays Mikael Blomkvist. Now that is an ingenious fantasy: a young woman with an attractive, virile, protective dude as an obliging junior partner and also a passive sexual object. Lisbeth has the feeling of a character who inspires emulation. In time to come, we will no doubt see as many Lisbeth clones as Spade and Marlowe inspired in their time.

FANTASY OR NOT, EVERY CHARACTER must have a backstory.

A past.

Chief amongst the basic truths of storytelling is the one that maintains that you must start as close to the end as possible. It is a common beginner's error to start his story far too early in the character's development. A character's backstory may only appear in flashback or be referenced once or twice in dialogue but it contains the important events in his past that allow the character to react as he does.

As an example, let's once again consider the character of Jake Gittes, in *Chinatown*. Before the story starts, he has retired from the LAPD and become a private dick after a tour of duty in the city's Chinatown has resulted in the death of a woman he loved; he is haunted by the guilt he feels about her demise.

A Caucasian cop never knows what's really going on in mysterious Chinatown; L.A's corrupt Anglo business and political establishment as represented by the Huston and Dunaway characters will prove to be equally impenetrable for Gittes.

"You may think you know what you're dealing with, but, believe me, you don't."

Assigning a dramatic past like this to your lead character is essential; without the backstory, he or she has no depth and the audience will experience them as cartoons. Flashbacks, however, are best kept to a minimum; a couple lines of dialogue are usually sufficient.

For similar reasons, your major characters must all have strong values. Not necessarily good or worthy values (the mean streets and what he's had to do to survive there have corrupted Alonzo Harris) but like Spade, he must have a code, the code of the street narc, the fine points of which he spends the movie propounding.

"Cover your area, cover your ass, but not necessarily in that order, right?"

In *Almost Famous*, written and directed by Cameron Crowe, the veteran rock journalist Lester Bangs, played by Philip Seymour Hoffman, tells the teenage tyro, William Miller, how to behave when he goes out on the road with rock celebrities. They're not your friends, he explains. Rock stars, he says, want you to write sentimental puff pieces about the genius of what is essentially dumb, glorious teen music. In fact, Crowe is establishing a set of values: the traditional code of the reporter.

"You should build your reputation on being honest and unmerciful."

Every occupation or profession has its code: somewhere in your script, you must articulate it. Similarly, every occupation has its inner stresses and conflicts. Therein lies the drama. The Ages of Man, from youth to senility are not professions but they too have their characteristic dramas of identity.

Since most feature films are aimed at an adolescent audience, no matter the genre, the coming-of-age drama is always the emotional subtext. In their separate ways, *Juno, Training Day,* and *Almost Famous* are all coming-of-age stories. All three concern young people trying to discover their own ideas and values in the face of a complex adult society.

Back to family values.

Coming of age.

Jesus! The psychic motherlode of modern day screenwriting.

In order to mine this motherlode, the aspiring screenwriter must understand adolescent psychology better than any shrink. Extroverts in the movies make for strong drama because they act out. Introverts are better suited to the novel. Paranoids make for strong characters because they're aggressive.

If the psychic concerns of the present-day cinema audience are essentially adolescent, those of the cable television audience are more adult because that's who's watching. Just the same as any teenager, the adult audience wants to see themselves and their emotional concerns up there on the screen.

Work, family, money, illness.

The protagonists of the HBO Sunday-night series *The Sopranos, Deadwood,* and *Boardwalk Empire,* even though they are portrayed by markedly different actors, created by different writers, are essentially the same character: Big Daddy under siege. The conflict entirely concerned with the fight for power.

As a character, the mob boss has an enduring fascination. Like a royal in Shakespeare, he rules an essentially medieval kingdom based on primeval loyalty and ruled by force. And the head that wears the crown is always uneasy. Yet, Big Daddy is our contemporary. And he's more compelling than the usual run of doctors and lawyers seen on television. Unlike that other figure of male authority, the private dick, Big Daddy looks down on his society from a lofty viewpoint.

If he's Al Swearingen, his antagonist is a mining tycoon like George Hearst. If he's Nucky Thompson, political boss of 1920s Atlantic City, he's fighting off Arnold Rothstein on one hand, and Harry Daugherty, Attorney General of the United States, on the other.

Both Al Swearingen and Nucky Thompson have crooked towns to run. Both Nucky and Tony Soprano are beset by family problems. Fathers and sons. No matter how violent their stories become, they are all essentially TV soap operas.

So, no matter how worthy your protagonist, the dramatist must make awful things happen to him, so the audience can see what he is made of. Otherwise, there is no drama.

As a character, Tony Soprano is well worth investigation. After all, he revolutionized television throughout the world. The series that bears his name was perfectly matched to the digital media revolution. The boxed sets of DVDs of *The Sopranos* created a completely new multi-million dollar market and destroyed the made-for-television movie in the process.

The character himself is a witty conceit: a Jersey mob boss who sees a shrink. As such, the character represents a dramatic paradox: brutal but introspective. At heart, Soprano is just another variant of that old standby, the whore with a heart of gold. He's a thug with a thirst for self-knowledge. Both characters are equally improbable. Soprano, thug that he is, also has a heart of gold, but it's reserved for his family.

The big lug loves his kids.

The big lug'll hang you up on a meat hook if you harm a hair on their heads.

Al Swearingen, Big Daddy gone West, is also possessed of a heart of gold. He is also a familiar figure from hundreds of westerns of the 1930s and 1940s: the saloon owner who the good guy marshal must defeat if law 'n' order is to come to the frontier town. In *Deadwood*, the saloon boss is the protagonist rather than the antagonist. Although he can be just as brutal as Tony Soprano, his loyalty is ultimately to the town itself. In his rough-hewn way, he too promotes the interests of the community in Deadwood. Al is one civic-minded pimp and murderer. As such, he is just as much a fantasy figure as Juno MacGuff.

To emphasize his essential nobility, Swearingen's dialogue is flat Shakespearian. In fact, the writer of *Deadwood*, David Milch, in order to portray the Swearingen's essential nobility, can be said to have reinvented stage soliloquy for our times.

Al Swearingen and Tony Soprano are the adults in the room. Increasingly, as the audience consists more of children and adults with a child's mentality, the screenwriter is called upon to create characters directed to a child-like sensibility – non-human beings from aliens to superheroes to vampires to anthropomorphic animals.

When inventing such creatures, it's important to empha-size the animal's human side. Movie dogs should be loyal and gentle, or exceptionally smart. King Kong is primitive, dark, and mysterious. He is not just a big gorilla: he is a 100-foot monument to repressed sexuality.

In the romantic, magical world of fantasy, characters may be evil, but never horrifying. Like King Kong, they may be oversized, or they may be diminutive, like the Seven Dwarfs.

To recap, the starting point in character creation is para-dox, a dramatic idea that combines light and darkness. The Phantom of the Opera is a beautiful generous soul inside a hideous outcast. Hannibal Lecter is a brilliant psychiatrist who happens to be a serial killer. Lisbeth Salander is a mental patient who is also a computer genius.

These characters are star roles. The actor who can do them justice will be a star, or will continue to be a star. If, as a writer, you create star roles, the earth will be yours, and everything that's in it.

CHARACTER RELATIONS

THE EMOTIONAL DYNAMIC that a screenwriter creates between his characters is just as important as the individual qualities and inner conflicts he bestows on them, and this dynamic goes a long way to define their personas. By throwing contrasting personalities together, the writer creates drama – and a new chemistry.

The writer's protagonist should have several levels of relationships, all of which serve to define his identity. The first level of relationship is with his allies and supporters. These are relationships of love or partnership. The second level is with his antagonist. The last level of relationship is with the supporting characters. This final stage of relationships serves to define the hero's connection to his world, his society – at large.

When creating relationships, romantic or not, the dramatist must give his characters something in common that brings them together and contrasting qualities that push them apart. Consequently, just as the characters themselves must suffer inner conflicts, the writer must give every major relationship in his story a dramatic issue, a *casus belli*. Otherwise, there will be no conflict between the characters and therefore, no drama.

But, just as there are stock characters, there are stock conflicts between them: fathers don't spend enough time with children, husbands don't listen sufficiently to wives, mothers are always pestering their grown children with phone calls, wives are shopaholics, etc. etc. Stock relationships and their issues, just as much as stock characters, should be avoided.

Nonetheless, when it comes to the first level of character development, as script consultant Linda Seger argues, partners with issues between them are omnipresent in contemporary moviemaking, not just in male-female relationships, but in relationships of all kinds: police partners, as in *Training Day*, husband-and-wife teams of assassins, like Brad Pitt and Angelina Jolie in *Mr. & Mrs. Smith*. Whether these partners are men or women, they all descend from the traditional buddy movie, where everything else, even plot, springs from the one central relationship.

The dramatic template for buddy movies of all kinds was established in that classic American genre of the outlaw couple on the run which dates back to the '40s.

Romeo and Juliet – on the run, down the highway, toting .45s.

Gun Crazy, Bonnie and Clyde, Badlands, True Romance, Natural Born Killers – these are just a few of the many lovers-on-the-run films.

The aspiring screenwriter does well to examine how the writers who invented these films' fugitive couples accomplished their task.

One of the very first of these lovers-on-the-run sagas, now mostly forgotten, was Nicholas Ray's *They Live by Night*, adapted from a Depression-era novel by Edward Anderson, and later remade by Robert Altman under its original title, *Thieves Like Us.*

Farley Granger, as Bowie Bowers, teenage bank robber, is the first incarnation of the Nicholas Ray hero, later raised to iconic stature by James Dean in *Rebel Without a Cause*. Like Marlon Brando's leather-clad biker in *The Wild One*, the persona Ray and his writers created for Dean, give or take a Jack Kerouac or an Elvis Presley, served as the model for the youth culture of the '60s which followed.

The Ray hero, whether portrayed by Granger or Dean, can be briefly defined: he's a mixed-up kid in a fast car.

Ray gives his bank robber hero a timeless motivation. Just like Mavis Gary and Roger Greenberg, Bowie Bowers just wants to settle down and have a life like anybody else.

But Fate won't let him.

Bowie, for instance, ends up gunned down by the law at the side of the highway in a motel driveway. Keechie Mobley, his Juliet, has been raised by an alcoholic father behind a gas station on a deserted stretch of Oklahoma highway. Bowie's a teenage convict who breaks out of the pen while doing a stretch for a murder committed when he was 16. Their relationship contains the dramatist's good old animating paradox: they are simultaneously killers and victims.

Once lovers, they are opposed by every one of the characters they come in contact with in the course of the story. Bowie's outlaw buddies, Chicamaw and T-Dub, just want to exploit him. The cops want to exterminate the lovers like rats, organized crime wants no part of them, and her family wants to turn them in for the reward. Every single one of the minor characters is venal and corrupt. Bowie and Keechie are screwed around and fucked over at every turn.

Doomed lovers on the road against the world.

All lovers feel that it's the two of them against the world. And the road has always been a metaphor for the journey of life.

In this early version of the lovers-on-the-run theme, Keechie stays away from the gunplay, stashed away in a series of motels; soon pregnant, she's the force pushing Bowie towards fatherhood and domesticity.

The evolution of women's role in society propels the evolution of the female partner in the relationship. Twenty years later, Faye Dunaway, in *Bonnie and Clyde*, occasionally is forced to take up the gun. By the time Juliette Lewis comes along in Quentin Tarantino's script for *Natural Born Killers*, she's enthusiastically spraying lead around with the best of the hard guys.

In its depiction of its central relationship, *They Live by Night* is a transitional film; looking back to the '30s and forward to the '60s. Bowie Bowers and Keechie Mobley are traditional *noir* characters in that they share the post-war disillusion common to the genre. Yet, in their relationship, the characters look forward to Ray's best-known film *Rebel Without a Cause* and the teen rebellion of the '50s where high-school outcasts James Dean, Sal Mineo, and Natalie Wood form a little improvised subculture in opposition to the mainstream of their families.

If his relationship with Keechie represents Bowie Bowers' better angels, that with his confederates Chicamaw and T-Dub mirror his darker, more violent self. Thus, Bowie's inner conflict is extended to these exterior relationships.

The differences in the relations between Bowie and his gang create misunderstandings between the characters, which create conflict, which creates the drama. Chicamaw Mobley, Keechie's uncle, is a hopeless alcoholic fuck-up, whose every move leads to trouble. Any venture Bowie might attempt with Chicamaw is doomed to failure. If Bowie is to survive, he must break away from Chicamaw or die with him.

T-Dub, for his part, only sees Bowie as a component of the robbery crew; for him, the kid's an afterthought. For him, Bowie's personal happiness is of small interest.

Yet, neither Chicamaw nor T-Dub cares to let Bowie have his life with Keechie in peace; they keep him wedded to their life of crime by pure force.

A lighter version of the lovers-on-the-run relationship is the bromance or buddy comedy such as *Sideways* in which Miles Raymond, played by Paul Giamatti, is a wine enthusiast, failed novelist, and impoverished elementary school teacher. Though he languishes in a small apartment, he drinks the best wines available, even if he has to steal the money from his poor old mom.

Needless to say, Miles is a nerd as well, unsuccessful with women, carrying the torch for his ex-wife, who's long since left him.

His buddy, Jack Cole, on the other hand, played by Thomas Haden Church, is a feckless womanizer, who's marrying purely for money, and whose shameless lies to the ladies lead the pair into evermore complicated comic troubles.

Like Bowie and Keechie, Miles and Jack are on the road, but the worst thing that's going to happen to them is a busted schnozzola at the hands of an angry woman, seduced and abandoned.

Although the romantic misadventures of a nerd is a dramatic cliché, the stroke of originality, in the case of *Sideways*, lies in giving the nerd, this time out, the occupation of wine connoisseur.

The character of a gold-collar worker like Miles is, in its way, as timely as a tech geek like Mark Zuckerberg. More than anything, Miles is a passionate consumer of fine wine. The craving for luxury on the part of those who can only occasionally afford it is the story of our era.

Their shared enthusiasm for wine is what Miles and Jack have in common. Their varying lack of success with women is what sets them apart and creates the drama.

However, when it comes to wine and women, Miles differs from Jack. He is a man with scruples, unlike Jack, who will drink anything, as long as he gets a buzz from it, and will say anything to a woman, as long as it gets him laid.

The buddy movie as a form is not restricted to guys like Miles and Jack. The most famous example of the women's buddy movie, of course, is *Thelma & Louise*, the 1991 feminist road movie in which a waitress and a housewife shoot a rapist and take off in a '66 Thunderbird convertible.

Like Bowie and Keechie, Thelma and Louise are just a pair of mixed-up kids with a fast car.

Women or not, the same dramatic requirements apply. Except for the pistol and the convertible, Thelma and Louise could be a contrasting pair of Jane Austen heroines. Thelma is passive and goofy; Louise is strong and stern. The sole difference is that, instead of making the firm choice between gent and cad, they drive over the cliff together in an act of women's solidarity.

Whether women or men, each character in the buddy duo, whether lovers or just friends, must also have the ability to transform each other for better or for worse, forcing them to change and grow.

As a general rule, your characters must be in the process of moral change, travelling from good to bad or vice versa; otherwise there is no character development and then, no drama.

So, in the typical coming-of-age drama like *Knocked Up*, the encounter with a Good Woman and fatherhood makes a man out of the bong-sucking man-boy.

Similarly, in *The American Friend*, Wim Wenders' German adaptation of Patricia Highsmith's *Ripley's Game*, the American, Tom Ripley, her charming psychopath, played by Dennis Hopper, transforms the good honest German, Jonathan Zimmermann, played by Bruno Ganz, into a hired killer.

Highsmith is far more than a genre thriller writer. Her highly distinctive stories, and the films made from them, are dramas of relationship and identity: personas stolen and exchanged. The chief emotion Highsmith creates in an audience is existential dread and paranoia. Ripley is in a constant state of terror that he will be exposed as a fraud and poseur.

Highsmith creates a unique character relationship between her impostor Ripley and the man who means to expose him. Ripley is cultivated and refined, all-but-European;

the debunker is always a coarse American bully. The debunker is the hunter; but the viewers are rooting for the prey. Highsmith takes garden-variety suspense and transforms it into existential dread, usually the turf of canonical authors like Kafka and Dostoevsky.

Parenthetically, it's instructive to compare the versions of Tom Ripley in the various adaptations of Highsmith's novels through the years. To begin with, Tom Ripley is a gloss on Henry James' character, Lambert Strether, in *The Ambassadors*. Strether is sent by Chad Newsome's wealthy father to Paris to rescue the poor lad from the clutches of a seductive Parisian woman. Strether fails in his mission; but he takes Newsome's lover and his lifestyle for himself.

In Highsmith's update of James, she ensures viewer-identification with Ripley by making him a lover of painting and, like Miles Raymond, fine upscale living. Ripley, when he is sent on a similar mission as Lambert Strether's, knocks off the prodigal son, Dicky Greenleaf, and takes over his identity, travelling the continent, living the European high life. The relationship between Ripley and Greenleaf results in an exchange of identities.

In *Purple Noon,* the 1960 French adaptation of Highsmith's novel, directed by René Clément, Tom Ripley is played by Alain Delon with effortless Gallic charm. With Delon as the hero, you're rooting for Ripley because he lives the spoiled and oafish Greenleaf's life of leisure with much more dash and élan than his loutish victim.

For the dramatist, how people like Ripley and Greenleaf influence each other in the course of a relationship is the most fascinating of studies. Does the bond between two people, whether friendship or romance, ennoble or degrade?

For instance, *An Education,* a screenplay by Nick Hornby, based on Lynn Barber's memoir, is a woman's coming-of-age drama. Jenny Mellor is a suburban English good girl, on track for a scholarship to Oxford when she is charmed away from the straight and narrow by yet another psychopathic con man, not American, but Jewish, which is possibly worse.

Jenny is transformed by her *homme fatal* from good girl into a bad girl high-school dropout. Her coming of age consists of learning the sophisticated ways of sex, art, travel, and fine dining at the feet of the caddish but charming Jew, David Goldman.

When Goldman, the bastard, turns out to be married, a sadder but wiser Jenny takes up her Oxford scholarship, now much better equipped for her career in the media. Goldman, who has seemingly degraded Jenny, has actually put her through Jewish boot camp, in the process ensuring her survival in the rough-and-tumble of life in the London metropolis.

Too often, the romantic relationship in a film is relegated to a subplot. Too many times, it is then played strictly by the numbers. The love interest is assigned what I like to call the "Don't-do-it-Joe" role. That is, whether Joe is about to invade Germany, fight for the heavyweight champion of the world, or just take a principled stand against the mob, the little lady is there only to say, "Don't do it, Joe."

Because it is so formulaic, the romantic subplot has been replaced in recent times by other plots concerning relationships with children or aging parents. And often enough in the age of family values, Joe doesn't take the big job as in *Moneyball,* climb Everest or step up against the mob, so he can dutifully take good care of Gramps or Sis.

Love relationships, needless to say, are a staple of screen-writing. The hero or heroine who has to choose between two potential mates is a dramatic situation that will be explored for as long as they make movies.

The purely romantic film, where the love relationship forms the central drama, however, also offers the hero or heroine a moral choice: dark and seductive bad romance or ennobling good lover. Consider *Pride and Prejudice*, Jane Austen's classic novel, dramatized in innumerable television and film versions.

Part of the reason for the perennial success of Austen's story is the way it combines the twin quest for love and money, for the greater good of the heroine's family, rather than selfish reasons. Virtuous, attractive Elizabeth Bennet must find a good husband to save the ranch. Darcy, every woman's favorite romantic hero, is a snotty punk with dough. In the course of the story, he turns out to be a stand-up gent. He learns how to apologize, something he'll probably be doing for the rest of his life, given Elizabeth's character.

Wickham, an early version of David Goldman, the bad guy, is charming, good-looking, great company and a great date, but – not to be trusted, as it turns out, with women or, much more importantly, money.

One of the reasons for Austen's perennial appeal is her understanding that character only reveals itself over time and that its revelation is the essence of drama. It's dramatic when Mr. Darcy turns out to be good. Ditto when Wickham turns out to be *baaaa-aad*. This human drama remains comprehensible to every generation, as long as courtship and marriage exist.

DRAMA HAS MUCH IN COMMON with song. In ancient times, they were scarcely separable. Popular song concerns itself with love won and love lost, mostly the latter. The love triangle has been a standby of both songs and drama for centuries.

Just as Cinderella is a sure-fire theme, as Vinny Lawrence once said, the writer has to be a hopeless klutz to mess up a love triangle.

Let's examine the relationships in one of the greatest love triangle films, *The Postman Always Rings Twice*, in its classic version with John Garfield and Lana Turner and the update, directed by good old Bob Rafelson and written by David Mamet, and starring Jack Nicholson and Jessica Lange.

Edmund Wilson described the James M. Cain novel as jungle lust in a roadside diner. Cain based his story on the real-life story of Judd Grey and Ruth Snyder, who got together and murdered Snyder's hubby in one of the most notorious murder cases of the '20s. Cain transferred the story from suburban New York and the middle class to the highway culture of Southern California and the blue-collar milieu.

Frank Chambers, whether portrayed by Garfield or Nicholson, is our familiar romantic tough-guy hero, now terminally down on his luck. Cora is a waitress in the shabby diner unhappily married to Gus Papadakis, its Greek immigrant proprietor.

Frank's a hard-nosed drifter with an eye on the main chance. Cora's a failed actress, just looking to settle down.

They're a couple of *dummkopfs*, equipped by Cain with plenty of human weakness.

It's Depression-era California.

The Production Code of the '40s prevented the original filmmakers from exploring jungle lust in its full glory but

Rafelson has Nicholson and Lange going for it ass over teakettle on the kitchen table, they're that hot for one another.

They both like it a lot.

But she's married.

That's a classic love triangle.

Observe how Cain turns these character relationships into the plot of a tragic drama.

As the novelist said in his *Paris Review* interview, you pull it, you switch it, you top it:

Frank and Cora run away together.

Doesn't work.

They return to the diner, decide to knock off Gus.

Doesn't work either.

They try to break up but the pull is too strong.

Frank and Cora try to kill Gus again.

This time it works.

They're immediately busted by the cops, the dopes.

In a split second, Cora and Frank rat each other out.

But:

They beat the rap with the help of a crooked lawyer. Like Bowie and Keechie, they live in a fallen world.

And this is the beauty part: *jungle lust turns to love.*

Frank and Cora settle down in the diner as all-American Mom and Pop. Cora is going to have a baby.

But:

Cora is killed in an auto wreck with Frank at the wheel.

They live in a fallen world.

Innocent Frank goes to the gallows for Cora's murder.

Jungle Lust and Violent Death: an unbeatable combo, boys and girls.

Lawrence Kasdan, in *Body Heat*, made an updated version of this love-triangle relationship, restoring its white-collar origins. But, in the age of no-fault divorce, killing for love is hard for an audience to comprehend. Why go to the bother when it's so easy to legally dump a husband or wife?

In an era where divorce is frequent and stable relationships not that easy to come by, a man who truly loves his wife and will do anything to protect their marriage is truly a hero in the eyes of a contemporary audience.

This is the theme of the British crime film, *Sexy Beast*.

Gary "Gal" Dove is an ex-con and retired safecracker, who has retired to a blissful existence in a Spanish villa with his beloved wife, an ex-porn star, Deedee. Together, they are trying to forget their Dark Past. Their beautiful life together is shattered when the raging sicko Don Logan appears, intent on recruiting Gal for a heist back in London.

When Gal and Deedee encounter Logan, the writers of the film have observed a cardinal rule of dramatic writing: namely, true love must not run smooth.

If the hero or heroine does not have a romantic rival standing between themselves and the beloved, the writer must find another obstacle to the relationship.

Although Gal, as written by Louis Mellis and David Scinto, is a much more engaging character than *Training Day's* Jake Hoyt, he serves much the same function as a point-of-view character. The character viewers pay to see is Logan, the towering violent psycho, as portrayed by Sir Ben Kingsley, all the way to an Oscar nomination in 2002.

Logan is possibly one of the most memorable bad guys in recent films. Kingsley described Logan as "the unhappiest man in the world." The writers, Mellis and Scinto, counterpoint

Logan's misery against Gal's blissful Spanish idyll. He is the violent, treacherous incarnation of the London underworld from which Gal and Deedee have escaped. Mellis and Scinto make Logan a rejected suitor of Deedee's best friend, Jackie. It is Logan's envy of the hero's happiness that sparks his spectacularly murderous rages. The story's violence emerges entirely from his relationship of envy with Gal.

After Logan hurls torrents of abuse at Gal and his friends, invades the sacred precincts of Gal and Deedee's bedroom, smashes a wineglass in Gal's ear and generally makes his homicidal intentions all too clear, it is Deedee who steps forward with the shotgun and blows the twisted fuck into bloody smithereens.

When push comes to shove, and home and hearth are threatened, it is currently Mom who should step forward and take care of business with the heavy weaponry and deal with the Don Logans, the obstacles that stand in the way of the happiness of Dad and herself.

In a lighter vein, the family comedy, *Meet the Parents*, and its several sequels, makes use of one of the hoariest of stock obstacles that stand in the way of true love, possibly centuries old; namely, the Disapproving Father. This character, down through time, reliably serves to keep the lovers apart. Greg, played by Ben Stiller, is a Jewish male nurse. Jack Byrnes, an upper-class WASP, not quite believably played by Robert De Niro, is the potential father-in-law who stands between Greg and marriage, disapproving as he does of male nurses.

Romantic comedies, like *Meet the Parents,* are a perennial audience favorite. Clearly more light-hearted than murderous love triangles, they offer a perfect diversion at the multiplex. Their most successful stars, such as Jennifer Aniston or Sandra

Bullock, each bear a distinct resemblance to the first 10 attractive women you might encounter at any suburban mall. They are the lowest common denominator made flesh.

If there any isn't any exterior obstacle to the lovers' happiness, the writer must supply the protagonist with an interior one.

For example, in *All About Steve*, Sandra Bullock plays Mary Horowitz, a comic female version of Mark Zuckerberg in *The Social Network*. Her social ineptitude stands in the way of her hilarious pursuit of the hunky CNN cameraman, Steve.

In *The Proposal*, Bullock's most successful romantic comedy, and one of the most successful romantic comedies of all time, it is the couple's employment situation that serves as the necessary dramatic obstacle to happiness. Cold and pushy publishing exec Bullock is handsome Ryan Reynolds' boss. In an age of workplace harassment regulations, how can she unite with the beloved assistant?

This bit of character invention is sheer commercial genius. It inverts perfectly the old *Cosmopolitan* magazine dream where the secretary marries the boss. Now the boss marries the male "assistant" and learns to be warm and caring.

Of all the character relationships in a drama, then, next to the hero and his buddy/lover, the most important for the writer to invent is that between the protagonist and the antagonist or villain. If the antagonist is weak, then the writer is denying his hero the chance to fulfill his role and become heroic.

In a sense, the relationship between protagonist and antagonist is an inverted love affair, a hate affair, if you like. Therefore, it must be given all the shadings a writer would ordinarily bestow on an affair of the heart. He can develop a grudging respect between hero and villain. He must show the intensification of hatred on either side; he can even create a false reconciliation, only to have the villain betray it, once again showing his true colors. Like the love affair, the hate affair between hero and villain must have depth, color and shading.

Accordingly, the dramatist must equip his villain with a view or opinion of the hero. This view can likely be mistaken or it can range from affection to grudging respect. Hero and villain can have a shared past, they can even once have been friends. In any event, you must give your villain a complex relationship to the hero. Otherwise the antagonist, too, will be composed of cardboard.

When films and television create bland heroes, their energies and sympathies are often directed to the antagonist. Drama, by its very nature, is profoundly subversive, despite all attempts to render it tepid. Lee Morgan, a jazz trumpet of the bop era, recounted how he was inspired by all those *bad hombres* of bland 1950s Westerns. Those bad dudes in the Mexican *bandido* moustaches and the black hats – usually played by Lee Van Cleef – who always hit the dust in Act Three, gunned down by the clean-cut hero, were the movie characters on which the bad dudes in the ghetto based their style.

Frank Booth, played by Dennis Hopper in David Lynch's *Blue Velvet,* is possibly one of the most frightening villains in film history. Booth is a violent, small-town mob boss, with a bad amyl nitrate habit and a taste for torture and rape. An S&M creep, he's given to crying jags, especially when he hears songs by Roy Orbison. He also enjoys calling his rape victims "mommy."

Now, let's just step back and examine what makes Frank Booth such a memorable creation. First, there's the laughing gas he whiffs from a portable tank; much more original than mere cocaine. More important are the public crying jags Lynch has given his character. They serve to convince us that Frank Booth is the very definition of a sick fuck, way out of control, in a very spooky way. Rage is a standard component of villainy: but teary, childish outbursts? That sets a new standard for the sinister.

In his later career, Hopper turned Frank Booth, the bad guy with the screw loose, into a cottage industry, playing that character again and again, becoming so wealthy in the process; he went from hipster to Republican.

THE COEN BROTHERS' *A SERIOUS MAN* gives us another type of antagonist, the despicable Sy Ableman, the faculty lounge Iago. In the Coen Brothers' continuing depiction of divorce, American-style, this guy represents the perfect incarnation of unctuous professorial treachery.

Ableman is screwing the wife of the movie's hero, the physics prof from Minneapolis, his academic colleague, Larry Gopnik. With his rabbinical beard and black heavy glasses, Ableman looks like an anti-Semitic caricature from *Der Stürmer*. Another pretentious wine connoisseur, he is the world's worst dresser, partial to powder-blue leisure suits.

Together with Larry's stolid wife, Judy, Ableman is scheming to move Gopnik out of the matrimonial home, and himself in. A man of patently false warmth and empathy, he is at once Larry's victimizer and his grief therapist. With the insufferable Ableman, bearish hugs are always on offer, even though he's probably sending anonymous letters to Larry's tenure committee behind his back, denouncing the poor schmuck.

Together, the slimily manipulative Ableman and Judy Gopnik earnestly explain to Larry that moving out of the house and into a motel is the adult, responsible thing to do.

"Larry, think of the children."

Ableman is a man you love to hate, big time.

When the Coen Brothers kill off the detestable Ableman in a freak auto accident, the audience wishes he had died more painfully.

Strung up on a meat hook, perhaps.

Because an antagonist like Ableman is the writer's second most important character, he too must be provided with values and aspirations. After all, nobody thinks of himself or herself as a bad guy. Nobody's purely bad. They're only acting for the greater good; for success, for accomplishment.

Don Logan believes he's only acting according to the code of the underworld. Ableman really does believe he's acting like a responsible adult. The writer should give the audience some insight into how the antagonist sees himself, no matter how self-deceiving his logic.

"I'm doing it for the wife and kids."

The difference between the hero and the villain is that the villain lies, robs, cheats and kills in pursuit of his goals. The challenge for the writer is to show that his villain is robbing, lying, and all the rest of it in a fresh and different way.

The Silence of the Lambs is another good example of a nicely shaded character relationship between protagonist and antagonist. Hannibal Lecter is a sadistic serial killer but he is a brilliant shrink, too. Like Tom Ripley, he has a taste for the finer things. Jody Foster is Clarice, the trainee FBI agent. Lecter is Clarice's mentor as well as her antagonist, a sort of father figure, who teaches Clarice valuable lessons about her career and her inner self.

Of course, Lecter is a complete fantasy, about as authentic as Batman. Still, audiences can't get enough of the serial killer who's also a shrink. The movies love serial killers for a very practical reason; they give the audience several murder scenes in the course of a film, plus endless suspense. Combine this with Life Lessons from Lecter, a sort of predatory Dr. Phil, and the sky's the limit.

Once you've created the major relationships in the story, you can turn to the supporting characters. What's true for Jane Austen and Henry James is also true for the screenwriter. The supporting characters help the writer define some quality of the protagonist – like a lamp illuminating a room, as James put it.

Everything a supporting character says and does should be directed by the writer to reveal some aspect of the protagonist's character, if only by contrast. For instance, in *An Education,* Helen is a worldly London bohemian, Wise in the Ways of Men. Hornby creates this character, not just to educate Jenny Mellor on the topic, but also to highlight her virginal innocence in their exchanges. Helen's sexual experience serves, by contrast, to illuminate Jenny's blameless virtue.

In the 1975 version of *Farewell My Lovely,* in the second adaptation of Raymond Chandler's novel, and one much closer to the original text than the '40s original, Philip Marlowe interviews Jessie Florian, the lonely alcoholic widow of a nightclub owner.

Robert Mitchum, in many ways, makes a much better Marlowe than Humphrey Bogart. As written by David Zelag Goodman and portrayed by Mitchum, Marlowe is aging, exhausted, almost languid. In order to extract information about Velma Valento, the vanished chorus girl of the title, he feeds booze to the alcoholic old woman and gets drunk himself in the process. Chandler creates the faded Jessie Florian as an engaging grotesque in her own right but the character's main function is to illustrate the depths to which Marlowe has sunk, his sense of his own failure, and his self-disgust.

As a demonstration of how character creates everything else in film, the aspiring screenwriter has only to hear the languid saxophone that underscores Mitchum's every move in *Farewell My Lovely*. The music is the objective expression of Marlowe's exhaustion and disillusion.

Parenthetically, Gato Barbieri's yearning horn serves the identical function for Marlon Brando's aging stud in *Last Tango in Paris*. Bernardo Bertolucci's film represents the death of that romantic tough-guy hero, literally and metaphorically, at the hands of Maria Schneider's sexually free woman. Their relationship is a dance of death. The tough-guy character is no longer just exhausted; he is half in a coma.

The Marlowe character dominated his world; when Elliott Gould played him in Robert Altman's film of *The Long Goodbye*, he was bewildered by the society he confronted. By the time Bertolucci and his writers created their version, the Brando character had already become lachrymose, self-indulgent and self-pitying. The liberated *femme fatale* portrayed by Schneider only had to administer the *coup de grâce*.

When the writer comes to invent his minor characters, he must also calculate how they define both the hero and the villain. Business executives need assistants, juniors, and chauffeurs to show they are powerful men. Drug dealers need muscle, enforcers, bimbos – their position in life is not clear without them.

The writer must contrast these various attendants and minor characters with the hero. For instance, Michael Mann's heist films from *Thief* to *Heat* to *Public Enemies* are romances of cool professionalism, whether the hero is a cop or robber.

Mann's protagonist, whether portrayed by James Caan, Al Pacino, or Johnny Depp, are always experts at their dark trade, always at the top of their game. However, there is always one minor character, a member of their robbery crew, who screws up, and turns the heist bad. (Heists have to go bad. Just like true love, they must never run smooth.) For some reason, the screw-up always has an ugly name.

In *Heat,* the character is named Waingro. In *Public Enemies,* he is called Shouse. This screw-up character always compromises the operation by his lack of control over his emotions. This, of course, is in dramatic contrast to Mann's hero, whose point of pride is that he always has his emotions under control. The screw-up, like all minor characters, doesn't get much screen time. Waingro or Shouse usually gets one in the head at the hands of Mann's hero in the back of the getaway car.

Small matter; this minor character, like all his tribe, was only created to make a point about Mann's cool professional hero.

BASIC STORY SETTING

CHARACTER AND PLOT ARE inextricably intertwined, like words and music in a song. Just as songwriters can tell you that sometimes the music comes first and then the words, character and plot are often mixed when a movie concept first occurs to a writer. Nonetheless, as we have seen, creating character is the first task for the screenwriter.

Next, comes dramatic construction.

Now, dramatic "action" does not mean mere physical action, or hustle and bustle, neither is it commotion. A writer can put a shootout into every scene, blow up everything in sight and still lull the audience to sleep.

Neither is debate a dramatic action. Two characters arguing aimlessly is not a drama. Each scene in the dramatic progression must have a clearly defined outcome. Dramatic action means character development and growth. Every scene in a dramatic progression must alter the equilibrium between the characters; it must depict an event that changes their situation. And it must arise smoothly out of the actions that preceded it.

A dramatic action must also create an emotional response in the audience. The character's triumph or defeat must be felt by the audience to the maximum. We must identify sufficiently with the character to care what happens to him; it must affect us as if it had happened to ourselves. Classic movie structure derives from the three-act form of the "well-made" play — the staple of the commercial theatres of Broadway and the West End for decades, even centuries.

Like its theatrical predecessor, classic movie structure is an interlocking series of set-ups and payoffs. Nothing can be set up in the first two acts that isn't paid off in Act Three. Nothing can happen in Act Three that hasn't been set up in the preceding two. Every manual that teaches dramatic construction quotes Anton Chekhov at this point, so I will too: "If there is a revolver on the wall in Act One, it must go off by Act Three."

So, let's examine the larger strategies of creating a dramatic visual narrative. Lope de Vega, the Spanish playwright, said in 1609: "In the first act set forth the case, in the second act weave forth events so you can't guess the outcome, in the third, resolve these events."

Another way of putting it: In the first act you present a situation, in the second act the situation changes. In the third act you see the result of those changes.

Vinny Lawrence would put it still another way:

Get your characters into hot water, then, get 'em out.

The first act should contain 10 or 15 pages of set-up, 20 pages of complication, the second act 45-60 pages, and a shorter third act of 35 pages.

The first 10 pages are the most important. If your script is a form of audition, the first 10 pages, at best, are what any story analyst will read. If you haven't grabbed them by page 10, haven't piqued their interest, you will have failed. Your script will go back onto the slush pile. The second most important are the last 10. If a reader gets as far as the end of your story without losing interest and tossing it on the heap, those last 10 are the pages they'll remember about your script.

In the 10-page set-up, the writer establishes the dramatic situation, the tone of his story, where it's located, and introduces the major characters.

The classically structured movie characteristically begins with images or an action scene, a major event, not dialogue.

A murder, a coronation, a robbery.

Often, the events in establishing action are much smaller. *Rob Roy* begins with a down-at-heels band of kilted men loping through the highland landscape. *The Grifters* begins with Anjelica Huston getting out her car at a racetrack parking lot and walking towards the grandstand to place a bet. *Almost Famous* begins with a close shot of the young writer's hand, composing in pencil on a pad of yellow paper. Each of these purely visual images establishes instantly the character of the protagonist, their occupation and their milieu.

However, conventions and rules exist to be broken. Art is anything you can get away with. *Dead Ringers,* a film written by David Cronenberg and myself, begins precisely with a dialogue scene between the twins, Beverly and Elliot Mantle, as children. They talk about girls; their relationship with women will be the film's theme.

Any film, not just *Dead Ringers,* has a narrative rhythm. Beginning with a dialogue scene starts the film on the offbeat, and gives it a very modern kind of narrative syncopation. The conventional approach, with its purely visual establishing scene, gives the film an inescapably stolid rhythm, like a white audience clapping on the two and four to a jumping R&B tune.

Right after the establishing images should come "the inciting incident." This term, like the emphasis on establishing motivation, was introduced into the screenwriting lexicon via Method Acting and Konstantin Stanislavsky. This "inciting incident" provides the trigger that lets the rest of the drama explode into being.

For instance, in *Burn After Reading,* the inciting incident is John Malkovich being fired for his job for alcoholism. In *Sexy Beast,* it's Gal Dove hearing about the phone call from London announcing Don Logan's arrival. In *They Live by Night,* the inciting incident is the jailbreak that sends Bowie and his bank robber pals out into the world of the Depression.

The inciting incident is your dramatic point of attack, and as such should be chosen carefully since it is the hinge on which the majority of the following story rests.

There are many garden-variety inciting incidents. A new boy enters school or a stranger arrives in a small town. A young girl starts work at a fashion magazine, or the client comes into the private dick's seedy office.

Throwing a fish out of water is a standard strategy in creating an inciting incident. Clint Eastwood, in *Coogan's Bluff,* is an Arizona cop sent to New York City to collect a prisoner. *E.T.,* like many another alien, falls to earth.

So the story begins.

The strong writer brings something fresh to this introductory gambit. For example, Wim Wenders, in *The American Friend,* following Patricia Highsmith, makes Tom Ripley push family man Jonathan Zimmermann into murder-for-hire because he insults him at a Hamburg art auction. The movie's thriller plot follows entirely from Ripley's thirst for revenge for a minor social snub.

In this instance, Highsmith creates plot from character in original fashion: Tom Ripley is a psychopath of such proportions that he would ruin a man's life to get payback for a minor social affront.

A common error is to begin the drama too early in the hero's biography. The inciting incident should occur as late as possible in the story. Unless they're especially important, childhood traumas, etc. should be left to flashbacks or dialogues of reminiscence somewhere later in the screenplay.

Most important, the inciting incident and the set-up should ask a question which the writer will spend the rest of the movie answering. In *The American Friend,* Wenders asks the question: will Ripley push Zimmermann into the world of crime? Secondly, will he survive in that dangerous arena? The writer should make the audience share in the hope that the protagonist will achieve his goal or fear that the antagonist will prevail, in the most painful way for the hero.

In the first act, as soon as possible, this thematic question must be asked: Will Jake LaMotta become champ? Will Jake Gittes solve the mystery of who killed Hollis Mulwray? Will Jake Hoyt survive training day at the hands of Alonzo Harris?

If you don't ask the audience a question of this sort, in the clearest possible terms, at the outset of your story, you will never hook their interest. The story hook is crucial. Without it, the rest of your tale, no matter what else you do, will have been in vain.

Northrop Frye says that every story is either an ascent or a descent. So, once the thematic question has been posed, a dramatic narrative generally depicts the protagonist's rise or fall. A reversal of fortune is, by its very nature, dramatic. A downward slope of crisis can be used to reveal the protagonist's character under duress. So, tragedy and comedy move precisely in opposite directions. Comedy moves toward a happy ending, tragedy descends into chaos and suffering.

Without this rise and fall, the narrative is absolutely flat. This happens, then that happens, then the next thing happens, with equal importance but without drama.

Narrative flatness is achieved, more deliberately, in the '60s road movies like *Easy Rider*. The boys hit the road, then go to a commune, then they befriend a jailed, liberal, alcoholic lawyer, Jack Nicholson and so on. The road movie is the cinematic equivalent of free verse; it's a loose and forgiving form. But even road movies have to ultimately enliven proceedings with old-fashioned melodrama. In *Easy Rider*, the screenwriters, using drooling rednecks as the murder weapons, knock off Captain America and Billy, at the end of the road.

The European art film, and its British, Canadian, and American off-shoots, also displays a characteristic flatness, scorning rise and fall as corny melodrama and favoring a cool, minimalist narrative style. An art film like *Shame* generally is light on plot. The structure, like the road movie, is highly episodic, generally exploring one aspect of the protagonist's character, in this case, sexual "addiction." *Shame*, like *Easy Rider*, rises to a crisis in the last ten minutes. Both are, eventually, descents into Hell. Not even the purveyors of art films, except possibly for Andy Warhol, dare deliver a couple hours of perfect narrative flatness.

By contrast, *Hamlet* is a Hall-of-Fame example of classic dramatic construction. Shakespeare, greatest of all screenwriters, establishes his hero as Prince of Denmark. After he makes his father's ghost tell Hamlet that his uncle murdered him, Shakespeare ensures that everything goes downhill for Hamlet from then on. Hamlet's is a paradigmatic descent. His murdering uncle marries his mom. Then, the woman he loves, Ophelia, deceives him; his friends, Rosenkrantz and Guildenstern, rat him out. Shakespeare makes sure everything is rotten in the state of Denmark, and that the time is way out of joint. The Bard's dramatic question is: can Hamlet resolve his inner struggles, pull himself together and put it right?

The historian of drama can pinpoint the shift from the royal to the domestic in the late 19th century in Scandinavia when Ibsen and Strindberg invented their first bourgeois domestic battles between husband and wife. Beginning with these Scandinavians, dramatic focus shifted from the royal court to the middle-class kitchen sink.

The Coen Brothers' suburban domestic drama, *A Serious Man,* has precisely the same reversal of fortune as Hamlet, Prince of Denmark. Larry Gopnik is a professor of physics at the University of Minnesota, a husband and a father. His wife is leaving him, his tenure is threatened, and his sad sack brother goes on the lam. Professor of physics and Prince of Denmark both face a classic dramatic situation.

If your hero is going to fall, Professor or Prince, you have to establish the height that he originally occupies. And you must depict what force is causing his fall. Both Shakespeare and the Coen Brothers suggest that Malignant Fate is responsible for their protagonists' troubles.

Still, the struggle for power, whether in the Court of Denmark or the University of Minnesota, is a primal human subject and thus perennial fodder for drama. Bada-boom-bada-bing Tony Soprano, mob king of New Jersey, or corrupt political bosses in *Boardwalk Empire*, or overreaching tycoons like *Chinatown's* Noah Cross, replace Shakespeare's royals.

If, on the other hand, your hero's narrative trajectory is going to be on the rise, then you have to establish the humble origins. All the dramas in the *Rocky* mode are Horatio Alger success stories, an upward trajectory of the hero's fortunes. But, just as lovers must be kept apart until the end in a romantic drama, the hero must be kept from his triumph in the *Rocky* style of story. The writer must invent as many obstacles as possible to throw in his path and dole out his portion of suffering. Rocky must lose a big fight in Act Two; Elvis Presley's rock 'n' rollin' King Creole must lose his gig at the club, all the better to triumph in Act Three.

Losing the fight, getting canned from the club, being dumped by Ophelia, provokes a crisis in anybody's life. Drama is the art of crises. A movie is an ascending arc of crises and conflicts, ascending in intensity and scope from beginning to end in a tightly connected scheme.

Now, here is exactly where character joins indivisibly with plot.

As we have noted, the most important aspect of character is motivation. What the character wants is what will drive him through the script. The more powerful his desire, the more powerful your story.

A dramatic crisis is created by the gap between what he wants and who or what's stopping him.

These dramatic crises must always intensify: you can never return to a previous level of conflict. Insults must inexorably rise to fisticuffs must rise to gunplay.

For instance, in *Training Day*, Alonzo forces Jake Hoyt to smoke weed laced with PCP, then to steal a drug dealer's money, a crime for which he plans to have him take the fall. Then, when Jake refuses to play along, Alonzo sets him up to be murdered himself. After the writer's made Alonzo force Jake to steal the dealer's money, he can't just have him smoke some more weed. He must intensify Jake's bad day in an ever-ascending scale.

At this early stage, the writer must identify the central conflict of his story. All else in his drama will revolve around that. And he must aim his story towards a third-act climax where the conflict will reach its highest point.

For example, the highest dramatic point of *Sexy Beast*, as in most heist stories, is the vault robbery in the third act. Yet, as strong as the movie is, it suffers because the writers killed off the villain, Don Logan, three-quarters of the way into their story. The confrontation between Gal and Don is the central conflict of the drama. Their climax isn't as powerful as it might be because, once the terrifying Logan has hit the dust, we, the audience, are not as engaged in the outcome. The ultimate test between Gal and Don comes too soon in the story in order for the central conflict to reach a decision that satisfies us.

This central conflict should determine whether the protagonist is the master of his fate or is unable to cope with "the slings and arrows of outrageous fortune." This conflict of wills between hero and villain must be strong enough to sustain and develop the conflict to a point where issue is decided. If either protagonist or antagonist has a weak will, then the drama itself will be weak and will fail to reach a climax intense enough to satisfy the audience.

However, the failure of a protagonist with a weak will, as John Howard Lawson argues in *Theory and Technique of Playwriting and Screenwriting*, to adjust himself to an inhospitable environment contains the elements of poignant drama.

In the 1934 adaptation of Somerset Maugham's *Of Human Bondage*, the hero, played by Leslie Howard, is a perfect English gentleman, betrayed repeatedly by a slatternly cockney waitress, played by the great Bette Davis.

Every time Davis comes back into Howard's life and ruins it, we feel sorry for the poor bastard. Maugham, and his adaptors, create emotion in the audience. Each of these dramatic crises is inextricably linked to the sado-masochistic character relationship between Howard and Davis.

Let's return to the beginning for a second.

If Act One sets forth the dramatic situation, the second act consists of complications. By this point, you have introduced the characters, hooked the audience with a question. The writer's protagonist must have clearly stated his goal and made clear how he plans to go about getting it.

And while you're at it, he should, at this point introduce the sub-plot, a subsidiary second story line. In my screenplay of *Casino Jack*, the main plot shows us Jack Abramoff's swindling of the Indian casinos. The subplot then portrays Abramoff's attempt to become the owner of his own floating casino. Eventually plot and subplot dovetail but the end of Act One is the correct spot to set the latter in motion.

Now, you should start throwing obstacles in your protagonist's way. So, the second act is the antagonist's showplace. It is here that the bad guy really gets to strut his stuff. If the hero can achieve his goal too easily, once again, there is no drama. In the second act, the hero often fails, so in Act Three, he can ultimately triumph.

If the story is a reversal of fortune, it is here in the second act that your hero should put up a fight. If he slides into death and destruction too easily, there is also no drama.

It's also important in the second act that you bring the protagonist and antagonist in close proximity so that they have plenty of opportunity to clash. So, you bring James Bond to the island of Dr. No, you put your commando team behind enemy lines, your detective should approach closer to the heart of the mystery, interviewing witnesses, identifying the suspects, getting derailed by false leads, and usually getting beat up for his pains.

Act Two is also a good time to set up the ticking of the clock, the period within which the hero must accomplish his goal. The ticking clock adds urgency and suspense to the drama and intensifies it.

Act Three is the last climactic 30 minutes of any film.

In most movies, the climax answers the question that the writer has posed with his inciting incident. More sophisticated films, in the European style, can dispense with the answer and end with another question.

For instance, *No Country for Old Men,* the Coen Brothers' film, based on the novel by Cormac McCarthy, ends with famous ambivalence. In Act Three, weather-beaten Sheriff Ed Tom, played by Tommy Lee Jones, instead of going for the final showdown with the psycho hit man, Chigurh, played by Javier Bardem, who he has been tracking for the whole story, just gives up the chase and retires on the spot. Now, John Wayne never would've backed down from a showdown with Anton Chigurh, but Tommy Lee Jones, by doing so, has allowed the Coen Brothers to ring some original character changes on the genre requirement of the western that lawman and gunman shoot it out in the final five minutes of the movie.

Ol' Tommy Lee is dam' tired.

South Texas is no country for old men.

One of the cardinal rules of classic screenwriting is that you can't take the final outcome out of the hands of your protagonist. According to Robert McKee, you must avoid the *deus ex machina*. This phrase comes to us via Horace, who in his *Ars Poetica*, counsels poets not to use the god from the machine. (In Greek drama the gods were often lowered down from the rafters by crane so they could settle the outcome.)

Of course, just as the Cubists violated the rules of perspective to their modernist purpose, screenwriters can violate the conventions of classic drama, provided that they know what they are in the first place. Every genre from thriller to western to stoner comedy to science fiction has its distinctive structural requirements. If your script doesn't meet those particular requirements, it won't be a viable blueprint for a film of the genre. If the story *only* meets the genre requirements, be prepared for it to be called, "formulaic."

In *Training Day,* Alonzo and Jake have a final showdown but it's inconclusive. Then the Russian mobsters, who we have been told are gunning for Alonzo, come along and wipe him out with AK-47s at a stoplight. It's not quite *deus ex machina,* since David Ayer has set up the Russians earlier in the story. But he has taken the outcome out of the hands of his protagonist, Jake.

If *Training Day* had been written in the '70s, Jake would have gunned down his boss, flipped his badge on the sidewalk and hit the road. But, in the time of the Father of a Shortstop, this isn't possible, if you want to keep the audience on your hero's side, so the gods, or the Russian mob, take your pick, come down and do the job for you.

(Many writers are so eager to paint their heroes as inoffensive that great squads of villains meet their ends conveniently slipping on grease spots at a great height or impaling themselves on fortunately placed iron fences: anything to avoid aggressively hostile action on the part of the protagonist.)

Before the mystery thriller disappeared as a feature film genre, there were interesting examples of writers and directors fooling with genre requirements in their approach to Act Three.

As we saw with the classic mystery thrillers, *The Maltese Falcon* and *The Big Sleep,* the detective, like Hamlet, brings order to a disordered world by solving the crime and bringing the criminal to justice.

However, in *Night Moves*, a revisionist thriller directed by Arthur Penn, the detective, played by Gene Hackman, only makes things worse for his clients, creating more disorder and chaos in his world. In Robert Altman's updated version of Chandler's *The Long Goodbye*, Elliott Gould's traditional private dick, Philip Marlowe, is completely baffled by the cultural revolutions of the '60s and travels across L.A. muttering dazedly to himself in response to a world that has passed him by.

Okay with me.

In his third act, Altman also tweaks the conventions of the buddy film. Marlowe is betrayed and played for a patsy by his only friend, Terry Lennox, played by ace right-hander Jim Bouton. Marlowe, after he's discovered the truth, tracks

Lennox down in Mexico where he's kicking back with his ill-gotten gains, and guns his back-stabbing former buddy down.

As for character development, the third act should ultimately reveal the fundamental nature of the antagonist. In *Chinatown,* John Huston's robber baron, Noah Cross, is exposed not only as the rapist of the land but of his own daughter, not to mention the father of their incestuous child. The screenwriter, Robert Towne, gives us a truly horrifying vision of ultimate evil, far more sinister than any lizard-like Alien baring bloody fangs, because Cross is more humanly plausible in his lack of moral boundaries.

Yet, even ultimate evil has its reasons. If, like Cross, you own the law, if you *can* get away with incest and murder, what's to stop you? As he tells Gittes, it's a question few people on earth ever need to ask themselves.

On a less tragic note, the antagonist can be revealed to have a human side. In *The American Friend,* Wim Wenders has Tom Ripley go to the aid of Jonathan Zimmermann, when his final hit-man assignment goes wrong. In this case, the antagonist ultimately befriends the protagonist. The hate affair has a happy ending. All is sweetness and light at the finish. It was Dostoevsky who said that even the wicked are much more naïve and simple-hearted than we suppose.

(In the case of *The American Friend,* by Act Three we also feel a political allegory floating to the surface. European political anxieties lurk under the crime film plot and characters. Dennis Hopper, in his cowboy hat, may well be America personified. Bruno Ganz may be Europe. Is America finally Europe's friend or enemy? Wenders opts for Euro-American friendship.)

The final scene must be a visual representation of the answer to the question asked in the first act. If the heist is a success, you see the robbers enjoying the fruit of the spoils. If not, the final scene will take place in the pen. If your story is a power struggle, then the victor is ensconced on his throne, whether literal or symbolic.

The challenge in writing strong third acts is identical in nature to many other screenwriting issues; namely, how does the screenwriter ring an original change on types of scenes the viewers have witnessed literally thousands of times? A romantic comedy must end with a wedding or some other scene showing that the lovers have ended up in each other's arms. If you tackle this scene head-on and just show the wedding, the certain audience response will be yawns.

So, you might set the scene at the preparations for the wedding and only show the couple at the altar in the final shot. Conversely, you might show the couple coming out of the church and driving away; anything to avoid the wedding itself.

Often, the location of the final scene is one we have never seen previously in the film. The dramatic and emotional peak the story reaches should have a visual correlative in the film's imagery. Perhaps the greatest example of this is the famous conclusion to *White Heat,* starring Jimmy Cagney. Cody Jarrett is an unhinged killer with a mother-obsession that won't quit. After, yes, a failed heist, he flees to the top of a gigantic chemical plant gas tank. When Cody meets his final doom, Cagney yells, "Made it, Ma! Top of the world!" Then the gas tank goes up in a colossal explosion.

That's hard to top as a movie ending.

STORY STRUCTURE:
CLASSIC AND MODERN

DEAD RINGERS WAS A SCRIPT that I wrote, my part of it, at least, purely on instinct. After the film appeared in theatres – it was number one in America for a couple weeks – the screenplay was called a "perfect example of dramatic construction" by the *New Yorker.*

I was later sent by a television network on a course given by one of those peripatetic instructors in story structure. There, I found out what David Cronenberg and I had done, without thinking at all about dramatic theory.

Dead Ringers does break with convention by opening with a dialogue scene. But, in several ways, it follows the classic progression of drama.

Here is a scene breakdown, showing how the film meets all the requirements of dramatic construction:

OPENING IMAGE. The identical twin brothers Elliot and Beverly Mantle, growing up in humble circumstances, precociously talk medical science to one another. They are eerily close, sharing every detail of their lives.

THEME STATED. The twins make a fumbling advance to a neighbor girl who angrily rejects them. A woman will be their downfall.

SET-UP. Elliot and Beverly, inseparable medical geniuses, grow to spectacularly successful adulthood as a team of high-flying gynecologists, specializing in women's fertility. The key to their brilliant success is a set of surgical instruments they have designed themselves. Beverly is scholarly and reclusive. Elliot is attractive and persuasive. They share an almost telepathic sense of communication; they even have a private language. Bev is awkward with women; Elliot is a lady's man. Cronenberg was eager to differentiate the Mantle twins from the usual doctors on TV so we made Beverly and Elliot almost as much creative artists as they were medicos.

INCITING INCIDENT. Claire Niveau, a charming, raffish actress with a taste for pharmaceuticals and kinky sex, comes to them hoping to cure her barrenness. As is their perverse custom, Elliot impersonates Beverly during the examination, so he can get a better look at her intimate parts. Because her reproductive organs are so strangely shaped, Claire can never have children but Elliot nonetheless begins a relationship with her.

CATALYST. Elliot, believing that his relationship with Beverly depends on their sharing everything, encourages Beverly to impersonate him in the affair with Claire. Beverly falls for her, hard.

QUESTION. Can Elliot and Beverly survive their relationship with Claire?

Once I'd decided on the love triangle, certain obligatory scenes sprang to mind, almost automatically. It followed that you would see the twins impersonating each other with Claire. You would then have to see her discovering that she was seeing two men.

TRANSITION TO ACT TWO. Elliot, the shallow lady's man, breaks off with Claire when she becomes too emotionally demanding. Beverly is devastated. He starts to see her on his own. The indissoluble union of the twins has been broken.

(The transition between acts must be accomplished seamlessly; there must be no gap in the narrative progression. A story hole, a set-up that isn't paid off, or, vice versa, a story beat that isn't set up and comes out of nowhere is, in the jargon of the D-girls, said to "bump." When the movie bumps and stutters, the audience flinches, and squirms in its seat or changes the channel.)

In *Dead Ringers,* the situation has changed.

ESTABLISH THE SUBPLOT. Raffish Claire hustles Beverly for prescription drugs. Addiction is catchy; he begins to develop a nasty little habit himself. The phrase that best describes a subplot is "the plot thickens." The writer uses it to create complexity and texture. However, it must be organically connected to the main plot.

Often, the romance provides an inadequate subplot, especially when it seems vestigial and throwaway.

ACT TWO – COMPLICATIONS. At this point, it's necessary for the writer to begin to answer the question he asked in Act One.

To the question, can the twins survive the love triangle with Claire, our answer is, "Hell, no."

Beverly passes on Claire's drug addiction to Elliot. Their medical practice starts to suffer as Bev starts brutally fumbling patient examinations and Elliot behaves erratically in front of the medical community at a celebratory professional gathering.

Under the influence of drugs, their technical brilliance in the design of gynecological instruments becomes warped and perverse. With the help of a sculptor, Elliot creates a set of beautiful but deadly surgical instruments. These implements were very much a Cronenbergian contribution.

Some writers love complications so much, they never want to resolve them. David Lynch, particularly, in movies like *Mulholland Dr.,* just strings out the complications and multiplies them. That is his signature narrative style. The narrative strategy of many cable series such as *Deadwood* or *Boardwalk Empire,* or any soap opera, for that matter, is to string out the complications for an entire season of episodes.

MIDPOINT. In a rise-and-fall structure, this is where the fall begins. At lunch with a bitchy socialite friend, Claire discovers that she has been seeing two men, not one. Outraged, she leaves town for a film shoot. Bev, befuddled by drugs, mistakenly believes she's sleeping with one of the cast.

THINGS GET WORSE. As we have seen, the crisis must intensify, troubles must increase. Reeling from Claire's perceived betrayal, Bev develops one hell of a drug habit that co-dependence forces Elliot to share. As their addiction deepens, Elliot horribly botches an operation. (It must be allowed as how Bill Burroughs' junkie surgeons were a strong influence here.) Elliot has taken to wearing scarlet priestly robes in the O.R. and using the bizarre instruments he has designed on real, live women. The twin gynecologists have come to warily mistrust the other sex.

LOWEST POINT. Brought before a medical board of examiners because of the botched operation where a patient is killed, the twins lose their hospital privileges. Their medical license is threatened. Masters of self-deception, the twins tell themselves they are now going to devote themselves to pure research.

END OF ACT TWO. In an effort to cure Beverly of his addiction so that they can return to their former medical glory, Elliot moves him out of their luxury apartment with the designer décor and into their medical clinic. He's going to cure him of his drug addiction all by himself.

In less tragic tales, this is the point where the protagonist turns things around and starts to get the upper hand on the antagonist.

Not so in *Dead Ringers.*

ACT THREE – RESOLUTION. Instead of Elliot curing Beverly, despite his best efforts, the latter drags him down into the morass of addiction. Even though he is warned by a woman doctor friend to save himself, Elliot sticks with his twin brother to the grisly end.

The result of the situation having changed by their relationship to Claire is that they are both destroyed.

Inside their clinic, the twins descend into an unholy squalor of terminal addiction. Of course, for the purposes of drama, this slide into the grave must not go unopposed. Nothing, even death and defeat, must happen too easily. So, Beverly momentarily escapes the clinic to take refuge with Claire.

But, despite her entreaties, Beverly too is unable to save himself from the pull of the relationship with his twin brother and returns to the clinic where he finds a debauched Elliot has moved on from pills to jacking dope right in the mainline. And the crisis goes up another notch.

Joined together at the hip, the Mantle boys regress into a second childhood and finally an infantile state until Beverly ultimately finishes Elliot off with the grotesque surgical instruments, freeing him from the malignant fraternal spell.

Shock tactics, true. But it's the shock that gives *Dead Ringers* its power as drama. No artist can succeed without audacity. The impulse that must guide the writer is:

Wait until they get a load of this.

Shock tactics are useful in getting the attention of an audience. In order to break through that huge fog of information and entertainment that make up the media environment, the writer must take strong measures. The body horror that Cronenberg invented, almost singlehandedly, serves to wake them up. Remember McLuhan: Art is anything you can get away with.

FINAL IMAGE. Claire breaks into the clinic to discover the twins dead side-by-side. Beverly has killed himself by hypodermic injection.

The central conflict came to me with the force of life-changing inspiration:

What if twin brothers fell in love with the same woman?

The rest of the story followed by instinct and trial and error, until it just felt right.

Intuition has to lead knowledge of craft and technique, but on its own, intuition will flounder somewhere down the line.

These progressive stages of dramatic construction, however, can be formulaic if approached too literally. They are like the formal structure of the twelve-bar blues or the thirty-two bars of the American Songbook ballad. Louis Armstrong and Charlie Parker improvised on these musical structures in very different ways but they still observed the fundamentals of the forms.

Instinct can work for one project, as it did for us on *Dead Ringers*; but every story has its own unique challenges. Finally, instinct is unreliable. A career depends on craft and the ability to keep abreast of the evolution of the screenplay form, which is continually changing, according to the changes in media technology, and the evolving psychology of the audience. (According to the aesthetic theorist Kenneth Burke, dramatic form is, in fact, nothing but the psychology of the audience.)

In any event, the various media are always cross-pollinating one another. Continuing hour-long series on television are frequently multi-character ensemble pieces with A, B, and C storylines. In one episode of *The Sopranos,* for example, you might follow Tony, Carmela, Uncle Junior, and Meadow, all in plot lines of their own. In addition, TV audiences often follow more than one program at a time, watching a baseball game, a news channel, and a drama, all at one time, with adroit use of the channel changer.

In addition, the audience is conditioned by their experience with computers and other digital media. Reaction time is speeded up. Films from previous decades now seem intolerably slow-paced. The audience can quickly pick up the drift of a story.

Because of these viewing habits, audiences are often bored with the conventional single protagonist structure in feature films. Following the fortunes of a single character makes them restless. The single protagonist story and conventional structure can seem simple-minded. A linear story is a straight narrative line and straight lines can be boring. So, the contemporary audience craves non-linear storytelling. As a result, in recent decades we've seen many example of the ensemble or multi-protagonist film. That is not to say, however, that they want incoherent story-telling. Clearly defined multi-character narrative presents a challenge for any writer.

In the '30s, stage plays, like Saroyan's *The Time of Your Life,* often used multiple characters, accompanied by a lot of Popular Front egalitarian theory condemning the single-hero film as *bourgeois*. Saroyan's play used a waterfront bar as a setting. Through the swinging doors came characters from high and low, rich and poor; the theatrical equivalent of a Diego Rivera mural. Multiple-character dramas are good vehicles if you want to explore society-at-large or social issues. Not so good if you want to explore psychological depth.

Films as far back as *Citizen Kane* and *Grand Hotel* have also used multiple protagonists. The *Kane* approach is useful if you want to explore a person or an event from multiple perspectives. *Rashomon* is the key example.

The '60s saw many bunch-of-guys-on-a-mission versions of this structure such as *The Magnificent Seven* and *The Dirty Dozen*. They were the inheritors of countless WWII films that featured a combat platoon with a Black, a Jew, a Southerner, and Italian, in a celebration of American democracy.

The contemporary form of the ensemble film can be said to originate with Robert Altman and *Nashville*. Since then, filmmakers as different as Quentin Tarantino, Atom Egoyan, and Jim Jarmusch have made extensive use of the multi-character structure.

There are several different varieties of this subform that the aspiring screenwriter needs to comprehend. Nonetheless, the beginning writer must master the conventional single-hero structure first, since the same fundamental rules apply to the ensemble film, as we shall see.

Nashville, although nominally concerned with country music, is mostly Altman's socio-political analysis of the psyche of an America that had seen the assassinations of public figures such as the Kennedys and John Lennon. Because there are more characters in the ensemble film, there is less plot than there is in a film like *Dead Ringers.*

The simplest multiple-protagonist structure is the dual narrative. In this genre, we track two protagonists, side by side. Unlike the buddy film, or lovers-on-the-run, which follows two protagonists together following the same story, these films present equally important but separate protagonists whose stories are running at the same time on the same theme.

Crimes and Misdemeanors, by Woody Allen, is a good example of the dual protagonist movie. Allen's theme resembles every cab driver's favorite lament: "Mister, there ain't no justice."

Allen is a true *auteur* in that, like his idol, Ingmar Bergman, he has remained a writer throughout his career. Many writer-directors discover that sitting alone in front of a computer screen is much less pleasant than working on a set with movie stars. Neither does the routine of festivals, press interviews, and the other activities required to promote movies encourage the introspection needed to write a screenplay. Since writing is a lot like playing the violin in that, unless you do it every day, your chops rust, it tends to fall by the wayside.

Like Bergman on his subarctic island, Allen has a taste for the solitude that goes with the writing life.

The two heroes of *Crimes and Misdemeanors* are Judah Rosenthal, a successful eye doctor, and Clifford Stern, a failed maker of documentary films. Allen's inciting incident occurs when Dolores, the doc's discarded mistress, tells him she intends to inform Dr. Rosenthal's wife about their affair.

Cliff, played by Allen, meanwhile, has been hired by his despised brother-in-law, Lester, a successful producer of schlock television, to make a documentary celebrating his life. The Allen hero is his standard wisecracking protagonist; Cliff is the comic relief, offering dramatic contrast to Judah's darker tale. Lester is the antagonist.

In the course of making the documentary, Cliff falls in love with Lester's associate producer, Halley Reed, played by Mia Farrow. Although he's dealing with dual protagonists, Allen sends them both through a series of ringing crises, just as in the single-hero structure.

Judah has his obnoxious blackmailing girlfriend knocked off by a hit man hired by his wise-guy brother when she threatens to expose his shady financial dealings. Despite a few heart-stopping moments, the doc gets away with murder; though he comes down with a nasty case of the guilt. These he shrugs off as easily as heartburn.

Halley rejects Cliff in favor of the despicable Lester because the jerk can help with her showbiz career. Just as their characters contrast, so do their plot trajectories.

Just like real life. Nice guys finish last. Women like a winner. The villain comes out on top.

There ain't no justice.

Allen's other multi-character film, *Hannah and Her Sisters,* as described by the critic Kristin Thompson, is especially instructive for the beginning writer. It's an even better example of how the conventional model of the single-hero form nevertheless underlies the ensemble structure.

In this film, Allen's theme is more profound than nice guys finish last.

In *Hannah and Her Sisters,* Allen's explores the unpredictable nature of love. There are five characters, whose lives are traced from one year to the next. Allen begins the story with one Thanksgiving party, where the characters are all introduced, and ends with the following year's gathering, when their lives have all changed.

The major characters are Hannah and her two sisters, Holly and Lee. Hannah's current husband, another Elliot, and her ex-husband, Mickey. Allen's film is a study of a showbiz family. The story revolves around Hannah, a successful actress, again played by Mia Farrow. As a character, she doesn't have much to do in the story, even though it's suggested that Hannah's acting supports the family. Nonetheless, as Thompson points out, all the other characters revolve around her.

Allen, at his best, is expert at creation of viewer-identification with the urban clerisy – all those lovable, neurotic professors, doctors, lawyers, film critics, writers and actors – and their folkways, especially marriage customs. The members of the clerisy largely identify with Allen's endearing movie persona and, although disapproving of his marital misadventures, they still adore him. His characters have the same sort of weaknesses they do and they can recognize themselves in his movies.

Allen's multiple characters, just like the protagonists of the conventional movie, have goals. In their case, because the characters are the sorts of anxious types who change their mind frequently, they happen to be shifting goals. Nonetheless, each of these characters' shifting goals is clear and thoroughly motivated.

Allen is the film chronicler of Starbucky people. His characters spend a lot of time talking about their attitudes and desires. Because his theme is the unpredictability of love, he necessarily spends a lot of time depicting the fragile and changing nature of family life in the modern era. Sometimes, Allen even glamorizes neurosis. To be anxious and depressed becomes a variety of intellectual credential.

(Now that insecure lives are the portion of corporate execs and professionals as well as showbiz and media folk, Allen's film has wider resonance. Large segments of the populace live in daily anxiety about their future. As one sax player puts it, these days we're all jazz musicians.)

Still, *Hannah and Her Sisters* is considered Allen's most optimistic, life-affirming film. Despite its themes of adultery and unstable relationships, it too is an assertion of family values.

SET-UP. In the ensemble film, Thompson argues, there is less time to deal with each of the characters, so each of them should be less shaded than a character in a single protagonist story. Each of them has one basic character trait or personal dilemma that will be explored in the course of the film.

Elliot, Hannah's husband, played by Michael Caine, wants to leave her for her sister, Lee. He proceeds to debate this issue with himself and his shrink. He can't make up his mind. Lee's most important quality is her beauty. She is attracted to intellectual men. She lives with Frederick, a reclusive, self-denying artist, who has ceased to attract her in bed or in conversation. Frederick, played by Bergman veteran, Max von Sydow, is a vestigial antagonist. He is such a minor character – and pathetic to boot – that he doesn't really deserve to even qualify as a villain.

Mickey, played by Allen, is, what else, a loveable hypochondriac, who once had a disastrous date with Holly, who herself dabbles in acting and a catering business, bouncing from guy to guy. All this is established at the Thanksgiving party or soon after.

TRANSITION TO ACT TWO. Holly's goal is to become a successful actress and find a guy. She finds David, an architect, briefly. He turns out to be fickle and the relationship ends. Lee's marriage to Frederick deteriorates. This jerk has so much false integrity he refuses to sell even one of his paintings. Elliot tells Lee that he is splitting from her sister and makes a move on her. She responds to him and waits for him to move out. He doesn't, so she breaks things off. Again, it's rising action, a series of dramatic crises.

There are fantasies and flashbacks. Mickey fantasizes that he's dying of cancer; we see the flashback of his awful date with Holly.

Then, the goals change. Because of his cancer scare, Mickey quits his job as a comedy writer and seeks the meaning of life. Elliot changes his mind about leaving Hannah. Holly changes her mind about becoming an actress and starts to write a play.

ACT TWO. Just as in the classic single-hero structure, the situation changes. There's a delay in the achievement of goals. Elliot's affair with Lee continues; he discusses with the shrink how she's different from Hannah, not as much as a super-woman. Lee is discovered to be having an affair by her husband. Here, Allen displays a great deal of insight into his characters. In a more conventional film, morality is clear-cut and adultery always leads to separation and divorce. Here, in moral shades of grey, Lee and Frederick don't quite break up, although they talk about it a lot.

Elliot discusses his feelings at great length; his guilt, his self-loathing. His goal is to make up his mind between Hannah and Lee. Mickey tries to find meaning in various religions and fails; he gets depressed.

TRANSITION TO ACT THREE. Time passes. Lee tires of waiting for Elliot to make up his mind. Holly's on the phone with Hannah. They talk about the arrangements for this year's Thanksgiving party.

ACT THREE – RESOLUTION. Lee breaks up with Elliot and starts seeing another guy. Elliot makes up with Hannah. Mickey has given up his quest for the meaning of life. He runs into Holly in a record store and they start seeing each other. They fall in love. By the time Thanksgiving rolls around, they're married and she's pregnant.

Life and dramatic structure are both affirmed.

Both *Crimes and Misdemeanors* and *Hannah and Her Sisters* are multi-character stories where the characters are bound together by their family connections. Different sorts of groups can also serve to unify a multi-character narrative. A sports team, as in *A League of Their Own,* is always useful. So is a class or a club, as in *The Dead Poets Society* or *Diner.* An anthology film such as *New York Stories* is a like a book of short stories: three unconnected characters, presented in sequence, bound together by their city. *Pulp Fiction* presents a group of interconnected characters but scrambles the time sequence.

An alternative narrative strategy can be created in a series of stories of unconnected characters, joined only by chance. Tarantino's influence has been worldwide, and we have seen Italian, British, and Latin-American crime films with non-linear, multiple-character stories.

The best of these films was *Amores perros* (*Love's a Bitch*), a Mexican film written by Guillermo Arriaga, whose contrasting rich and poor characters are only connected by a car crash. Paul Haggis' film, *Crash*, borrowed Arriaga's traffic-accident device and applied it to the perennial American theme of race, connecting black and white, rich and poor characters through the highly symbolic car-crash incident.

The Italian film *Gomorrah* is a multi-character crime drama where the five characters' stories are entirely separate, unified by a different sort of family connection, their involvement in Italian organized crime in the region of Naples. Its theme: the corruption of an entire society, high and low.

The narrative structure of *Gomorrah* is intentionally disorienting; little is explained about the Italian social context. Unlike the Hollywood approach, where the audience is spoon-fed, in *Gomorrah,* they are thrown into the chaos of Naples under the influence of the Camorra and left to sink or swim. Men, women, rich, poor, middlemen and higher-ups are only linked by geographical proximity. The movie is also distinguished by the novelty of the criminal enterprises it depicts: illegal waste disposal and the counterfeiting of designer clothing – subject matter considered prosaic by American filmmakers.

Multiple-character structure can be used to revive genres that have become over-familiar. For instance, the mystery whodunit, which had been relegated to television, found a new lease on life in feature films with the adaptations of *The Girl with the Dragon Tattoo.*

Lisbeth Salander and Mikael Blomkvist are dual protagonists, inhabiting separate narrative tracks until a point well past the middle of the story where they join forces. Not only is Lisbeth a gender update on the tired old male investigator, the film's structure itself seems more contemporary than that of the classic detective movie.

Films gain prestige by concerning themselves with the social or the psychological. Eventually, films that dealt with the depths of human nature would have to find a way to non-linear narrative structure. In the '60s and '70s, following Fellini's example in films like *Juliet of the Spirits,* extensive use was made of dream sequences and extended flashbacks interpolated with a traditional dramatic structure. With good reason, this strategy came to be seen as self-indulgent after too many uninspired dream sequences by Fellini's imitators.

Nonetheless, Terrence Malick, another writer-director with a taste for solitude, in *The Tree of Life,* offers the aspiring writer a new direction to follow if he wishes to explore the cutting-edge of the non-linear psychological film.

The Tree of Life explores the Texan childhood of Jack O'Brien. Mrs. O'Brien is spiritual and gentle. Mr. O'Brien, played by Brad Pitt, is a hard-ass who's disappointed in his career as an inventor and believes his sons need to toughen up. If the Father of a Shortstop is the hero of commercial cinema these days, the fascinating father, equally good and bad, is the dominant figure in upscale cinema.

Starting and finishing the movie with the image of a flickering red-yellow flame that possibly symbolizes the Divine

Spark, Malick intersperses scenes from Jack's Waco childhood with ones from his unsatisfactory adulthood as an architect in New York.

The biggest non-linear innovation is the second act interpolation of scenes from the birth of the universe – galaxies and dinosaurs – with the creation of Jack O'Brien's personality. Malick's depiction of the birth of the universe gives a new meaning to the concept of backstory. Creation's a backstory that goes *waaa-aaay* back.

If the beginning of life on Earth is not sufficient, Malick ends his movie with a third act flash-forward to the Life Eternal, where Jack is reunited on the Far Shore with mom and dad and his little bud who died in Vietnam – the news of whose death reaching Waco is, yes, the inciting incident of the movie. It's also hard to beat the afterlife as a fresh location to set a scene for the third act finale. Malick portrays it as a rocky beach looking out on the endless sea of Time.

It would be difficult for another writer to emulate Malick's non-linear, cosmic style without being derivative or risking absurdity. Nonetheless, his imaginative audacity in linking cosmic imagery to the personal life of the individual breaks new ground in visual storytelling.

Malick links character and plot in the persona of Mrs. O'Brien, who is profoundly religious, and who tries to show life to her children as full of wonder. Chief among these wonders is the personality of Mr. O'Brien, a hothead engineer, a Texas authoritarian who rules his sons with a heavy hand.

Malick is also given to shooting his characters against vistas of big sky, which has the effect of adding to the cosmic dimension of his story. He has also discovered a cinematic way of depicting psychological depth in post-Freudian religious terms. If there's a flaw in his narrative, it's that he fails to show what the effects of Jack's Texas upbringing are on his adult life in New York, outside of just brooding on it. Then, it's difficult to portray the dark complexities of a successful architect's life in the big city in the same sort of detail as Woody Allen *and* show the birth of the universe as well, all in a couple of hours.

Consequently, Sean Penn's role in *The Tree of Life* is vestigial. Although young Jack is nominally the protagonist, youthful Hunter McCracken is not the star of the film. Brad Pitt, who also made the film happen as its producer, is here the main attraction. It's a good bet that if Malick had not attracted Pitt with the originality of his screenplay, the movie would've never been produced.

Even more complicated than the multi-character structure is that which plays with a story's time frame, in flashbacks and flash-forwards. *The English Patient,* as adapted from Michael Ondaatje's novel by Anthony Minghella, is a good example. There are some 40 time transitions in the film as the characters move from 1942 forward to 1945 and back to 1938 and forward to 1944 and so on.

The film has a dual-character structure, featuring the gravely wounded explorer Count Almásy, played by Ralph Fiennes, and the Quebecoise nurse Hana, played by Juliette Binoche. Instead of parallel stories, theirs are linked by their nurse-and-patient relationship. In effect, the movie's a mystery without a detective. Minghella asks the question, "How did the Englishman get to be Hana's patient?"

Count Almásy's story is a love triangle, no different from *The Postman Always Rings Twice,* except for its silver-spoon setting amongst a Saharan archeological expedition and the fact that the husband conveniently kills himself. Hana is an anachronism; a modern-day liberated lady, looking for love. In any event, despite the dual-character structure and all the antics with the time scheme, Minghella's script still hits all the conventional story markers: opening image, inciting incident, first act, transition to second, etc, etc. The stakes are raised for the characters when war is declared. Nazis always serve as good bad guys and they obligingly are closing in on the Count by the end of Act Two.

Just like Woody Allen's, Minghella's theme is the unpredictability of love. Instead of the psychic battleground of Manhattan, we have the chaos of World War II. Although critics loved the movie, and it received many awards, the mass audience found the complex time structure too demanding and the movie disappointed at the box office.

In any event, the true hero of the non-linear film, time-skipping, multi-character or not, is the director. Even more than in the classic drama, the bravura cinematic gestures of the form make it a director's showcase. Many of the proponents of this structure are writers themselves, even if they occasionally enlist collaborators.

The non-linear film is a complicated technical form, with many interlocking parts, probably best not attempted by a first-time writer. After all, a writer must be master of his means. It's best not to attempt something complex that you're unsure of doing well. (Tarantino claims that, in *Pulp Fiction*, he and his collaborator, Roger Avary, first wrote out the film in conventional order, then just threw the pages up in the air. How they settled determined the non-linear structure.)

In any event, the beginning writer must think long and hard before deciding what form best suits what he wants to say about his protagonist. Most beginners strike out on their screenwriting journey without knowing much about the structural choices that lie in front of them, and story chaos is the result.

The European art film eschews these various forms of dramatic structure in favor of a flatter narrative style that favors a minimal plot in order to explore character.

Shame, a British film set in New York, written by Abi Morgan and its director, Steve McQueen, *(No, not that one!)* is a character study of so-called "sex addiction," an affliction that more traditional observers, the Marquis de Sade, say, would call erotomania. (It's a measure of the pervasiveness of drugs in society that most other vices are seen through the lens of narcotics addiction.)

Unlike Woody Allen-style nerds, the protagonist, Brandon, played by Michael Fassbender, gets all the women he wants and more, by the sole means of a fetching smile and a $100 haircut. But Brandon too, "can't commit." In fact, any scintilla of affection during sex results, in his case, in a deflated hard-on. In the current era, you know the character is doomed when he rejects the claims of family, in this instance in the person of his sister, Sissie.

The structure of a film like *Shame* consists in revealing, scene by scene, the depths of the Fassbender character's addiction and alienation. Unlike the Hollywood film, where a character must move toward change, usually for the better, in the course of a movie, Brandon's trajectory remains flat. That is, until his fortunes head inexorably downward, without much resistance on his part.

There was some surprise on the part of critics that an art film like *Shame,* with its minimalist esthetic, was a modest box-office success. It's at this point that the critics usually trot out the screenwriter William Goldman's dictum, "Nobody knows anything."

Guess what: sex still sells, especially if the filmmakers seem to disapprove of the movie's soulless encounters, when the erotic images have the glossy elegance of a magazine fashion spread.

SUSPENSE

BETTER THAN ANY OTHER MEDIUM, movies can draw you in and make you lose yourself in the story. Suspense is the device that makes this absorption of consciousness possible. Alfred Hitchcock, the Hall-of-Fame master of the medium, said that movies are just life, with the boring parts left out. Suspense is a familiar condition in anybody's life. *How's it gonna turn out?* is a question we're always asking ourselves.

Will he call?

Will she go out with me if I ask her?

The news of the day is a collection of unfinished anecdotes as well. Leadership contests, elections, sports, and foreign wars

– all possess the element of suspense. That's why network news has high ratings.

Character development shares many qualities with characterization in a novel. Dramatic structure in movies differs little from that of a stage play. Purely cinematic devices, however, best create suspense.

Montage, the juxtaposition of images on film, is the best contrivance ever devised for creating suspense. The beginning writer must learn to use it, especially in conjunction with that first mover of the medium, character.

For instance, we see a getaway car pursued by a police squad car. The chase has been used thousands of times as a medium for suspense. It will be used another few thousand times in the future. Our getaway car speeds through the streets recklessly, taking corners wildly. We crosscut from the getaway car to the police car. Then we cut again to something dramatically placid in contrast, say, a line of schoolchildren crossing the street.

Are the bad guys going to plow right through them? If they did, what would that reveal about their character? If the cops did, what would it say about their zeal in enforcing the law? If one of the bad guys swerved to miss the kids and was arrested as a result, we would have to think differently about him. Ditto for the cops.

Hitchcock used this basic technique many times in his movies. If conflict is the essence of drama, crosscutting is the essence of suspense. The trick is to let the viewer in on something that the characters in the film don't yet know about.

For instance, in *Psycho,* the viewer knows about the crazy mother before Martin Balsam, playing the detective, does. So, when Balsam enters that Charles Addams house, we know something horrible is going to happen to him. A character walking into a dark room where the audience knows something terrible lurks is the bread and butter of the horror genre. Somebody in the audience will scream every time the something "suddenly" pops out.

One of Hitchcock's favorite devices is to a plant a bomb in close proximity to his characters, add a ticking clock, and make sure the characters are unaware of the bomb and the clock ticking down. He also enjoys throwing in a twist so that the bomb doesn't go off. Sometimes, Hitchcock defuses the bomb and the characters relax, then… *POW!*

The ticking clock can also be enlarged to a cosmic level. This is the characteristic suspense strategy of disaster films such as *Contagion.* If a cure isn't quickly found by a certain date, the virus will wipe out the world. The same goes for earthquakes, tsunamis, ice ages and all the other disasters, including the nuclear. Add a ticking clock and count down –

Voilà, suspense.

In thrillers, suspense largely consists of the threat of physical violence and danger. Raymond Chandler famously said that any time the action lagged in a crime thriller, send a man into the room with a gun in his hand. Better still, stick the weapon into the hand of one of your major characters. The viewer will be on the edge of his seat, waiting for it to go off. Better still; show the guy holding it blasting somebody. The audience will be waiting on edge for him to do it again.

No Country for Old Men is a good example of how a weapon enhances suspense. Chigurh, the antagonist, played by Javier Bardem, does a lot better than a boring old .45. He wields a stunbolt gun, a gruesome piece of equipment used to neutralize animals' brains prior to slaughter. Before administering the *coup de grâce*, he plays with his victims' minds, with a lot of pseudo-philosophical double-talk about Fate. Every time Bardem lugs the stunbolt into the scene, the viewer is in a state of suspense because he's already seen what Bardem does with that baby.

The Coen Brothers crosscut between the hit man, played by Bardem, and a lawman, played by Tommy Lee Jones, and an ordinary guy, played by Josh Brolin, who stumbles on a fortune left lying around in a briefcase in a drug deal gone bad on the Tex-Mex border. The briefcase, full of money, is what Hitchcock famously called the MacGuffin, the thing that everybody's searching for that's the excuse for the suspense. It could be government secrets, or the Black Bird in *The Maltese Falcon,* the crucial piece of evidence in a murder trial, or a million bucks. In *Chinatown,* it's a person: Evelyn Mulwray's daughter, the product of her dark incestuous liaison with her father, Noah Cross.

In *Pulp Fiction*, the MacGuffin goes unnamed. Something in a briefcase that glows. It's a test of the writer's ingenuity to invent a fresh MacGuffin, one that we haven't seen before. It doesn't really matter what it is, it's only the excuse for the suspense.

Again, suspense works best with a minimum of dialogue. For example: cars stop at a traffic light. The light changes and they drive off, except for one. Why doesn't it move? We crosscut to the car: the driver's been murdered.

Suspense has been created and not a word said.

In *Hannibal,* one of the sequels to *The Silence of the Lambs,* we see Hannibal Lecter walking in a crowded market in a foreign city, shadowed by a scruffy assassin. Bit by bit, the killer closes on Lecter, they collide, and the dude goes reeling, clutching his gut. Lecter strolls onward, unperturbed. The audience is panting to know, *what happened?* What happened is the screenwriter has withheld key information, which he now proceeds to disclose. The killer's buddy rushes to his aid and discovers an odd, curved weapon protruding from his guts; the blood flows, the killer expires. One more use of the "reveal."

In point of fact, Edgar Allan Poe invented many of these thriller techniques in the 19th century. All they are, said Poe, is a story, or parts of a story, told backwards. Every story beat from the point where Lecter and the assassin collide is told in reverse order: thus creating the reveal.

In general, the challenge in writing screenplays is to know and observe story conventions, like the MacGuffin and the "reveal," then find a fresh and original way of using them.

Any good story contains some degree of suspense. A pedestrian thriller has only suspense and nothing else. It grips the viewer's attention for the couple of hours they are watching and are instantly forgotten. What makes for a memorable suspense film is the creation of character. We remember Hannibal Lecter, but not much of the suspense plot of *The Silence of the Lambs*. We remember Anton Chigurh and his ruminations about Fate, not the plot mechanics of *No Country for Old Men*.

In a suspense film, one question only is asked. In the detective thriller, the question is: "Whodunit?"

In the crime thriller, the question is, "Will they get away with it?"

In the course of answering that question, the writer must navigate a series of twists, turns, and reversals between antagonist and protagonist, each of whom must reveal something about their character.

In *The Talented Mr. Ripley*, Highsmith and the director, Anthony Minghella, create a wholly original form of suspense: the fear of exposure. Tom Ripley, the forger and impersonator, teeters perennially on the verge of scandalous exposure and social humiliation. Where the suspense in Highsmith is located in the possible unmasking of the anti-hero, Ripley, in Hammett it is to be found in Spade's unmasking of the *femme fatale*, Bridget O'Shaughnessy. For the screenwriter, it matters little who's stripped naked at the end of the scene. As Vinny Lawrence would put it, what matters is creating the suspense and drama of the "reveal."

The Coen Brothers' update on *True Grit* is a pure chase film. Mattie Ross and Rooster Cogburn just chase the bad guy, Tom Chaney (also played by Brolin), who killed her dad. Much of the suspense is located in the revelation of character of Rooster Cogburn, played by Jeff Bridges in the remake and John Wayne in the original. The suspense question posed about Cogburn goes, "Is he a garrulous boastful old drunk or does he possess true grit?" The filmmakers add the obligatory twist to the final showdown between protagonist and antagonist when Mattie goes sprawling into a cave full of snakes after she's dispatched Chaney. And, of course, Rooster comes up trumps in his shootout with the outlaw Ned Pepper.

No Country for Old Men, on the other hand, is a triple pursuit. Tommy Lee Jones chases Javier Bardem chases Josh Brolin. The film is a modern-day western. In the old days, the street of the Texas border town would have emptied. Jones and Bardem would have walked slowly towards each other, as the viewers gaped in suspense, ready to draw. The modern twist is that the showdown takes place in a cheap motel and Jones just walks away, but not before he walks into a dark room with a killer waiting, just as in any low-budget horror film.

The longer the writer can draw out a suspense sequence, the better. Sometimes, the entire movie is one long seamless run of suspense. In *Speed,* there's a bomb on a bus crowded with passengers. Unless the bus keeps going 50 mph, the bomb will explode.

That's the movie.

In *Duel,* Steven Spielberg's first effort as a director, a malignant trailer truck with no visible driver chases an innocent motorist.

That's it.

Simple concepts, but effective.

Thrillers are not the only genre that makes use of suspense. A man teetering on a ledge is funny; we laugh at his antics trying not to fall. In *10,* Dudley Moore is waiting for an important phone call. While he waits, he uses a telescope to spy on a beautiful neighbor across the L.A. canyon. He hits his head with the telescope, falls into the canyon, and misses the call. Following the woman to church, he is stung by a bee and crashes into a police cruiser. The dynamic is identical to that of the larger dramatic structures. Moore has a goal: answering the phone. Writer/director Blake Edwards poses a question: will he answer? Then, he throws an escalating series of comic mishaps in his path, each topping the other and creating suspense. Again, it's the sort of film sequence we've seen since the silents.

No worries. The audience is not composed of film historians.

The romantic comedy also makes use of suspense. The question asked is, "Will Jennifer Aniston or Sandra Bullock get the handsome, charming guy?"

In the romantic comedy *All About Steve,* the writers ring new changes on an old story by having handsome Bradley Cooper not return her affections and then have her stalk him across America, throwing in as many comic obstacles as they can dream up. The twist is, having finally got the dude, America's sweetheart lets him go, reasoning that if you have to stalk somebody, they're not really that into you.

Setting is a major factor in creating suspense. There's a strong reason why so many horror films take place in an old house in the middle of nowhere. In a remote location, there is nobody to help. Remote islands as a setting are a perennial favorite. *Shutter Island* and *The Girl with the Dragon Tattoo* are two recent examples.

The threat of danger, or jeopardy, as it's known amongst the D-girls, plays better in a remote location. It is also good if the person is especially vulnerable, preferably a woman. If you see the danger from her standpoint, her fear is transferred to the audience and becomes theirs. Only, they are safe in their seats, and can go home at the end of the movie.

SCENE, DIALOGUE, AND DESCRIPTION

IN PREVIOUS CHAPTERS, we considered the larger strategies of constructing a film drama. Now, it's time to think about the tactics of creating an individual scene.

The way you blend scenes in your narrative creates the narrative rhythm of the movie. If you want to create a slow, deliberately *andante* pace, many long scenes, back-to-back, will produce the desired effect. Conversely, a flow of short scenes will create a fast pace. Deft combinations of long and short create a syncopated kind of narrative rhythm.

Even in a traditional, linear structure, where the story is told more or less in straightforward fashion, it's best to vary the narrative occasionally by reversing the natural order of scenes, by flashing just slightly forward in the story. Otherwise, the narrative plods in bovine fashion.

For instance, in *Sexy Beast*, the writers depict the origin of the heist for which Don Logan is recruiting Gal, as beginning at an orgy in the naughty London demimonde, where the top and bottom of society get together to get off.

This sequence of scenes begins where it would ordinarily end, with black-clad gangster Teddy Bass, played by the saturnine Ian McShane, in the throes of some unimaginably perverse sexual ecstasy. The rest of the sequence goes back just a few moments in time to show how Bass came to be in such erotic transports. The viewer discovers how he met the decadent banker at the orgy, how they both hooked up with the hooker, etc. This minor flashback produces a narrative stutter step that adds complexity to what would otherwise be plain vanilla storytelling.

As far as content of a scene is concerned, what is true of the larger structure is also true of the smaller ones. The Aristotelian unities still hold: beginning, middle and end. You should begin your scene as close to its end as possible. A scene is like a joke: there's a set-up and a punch line; you need to go out strong.

A scene has to do one of two things, preferably both: advance the story and develop character. If it does neither, it has no reason to exist and should be cut from the script.

Just as there are different narrative rhythms, there are different styles of dialogue. The early talkies of the 1930s, influenced heavily by stage plays and radio drama, were dialogue-heavy. The screwball comedy was often nothing but scenes with witty dialogue. So were other black-and-white classics like *All About Eve.*

The 1960s were a visual time, so Sergio Leone's spaghetti westerns employ very spare dialogue, or often no dialogue at all, just expressive blinks, sneers, narrowing of eyes, etc. Films of the era, like *Bonnie and Clyde,* often dispense completely with dialogue for long stretches, running soundtrack music over moving images of cars or motorcycles.

In any era, the screenwriter must make an assessment of his or her strengths and weaknesses. If writing dialogue is not your strong suit, it's best to minimize its use, keep it spare. Then, it's definitely a case where less is more, and the more functional the better.

In the late '90s, dialogue made a comeback in the films of Quentin Tarantino such as *Pulp Fiction.* Now, producers in Hollywood call any witty dialogue, especially of the streetwise variety, "Tarantino dialogue."

Ironically, Tarantino's style of run-on dialogue has a literary provenance. Tarantino picked it up from Elmore Leonard, who was influenced by *The Friends of Eddie Coyle*'s George V. Higgins, who got it from John O'Hara, who in turn got it from Hemingway, who, amongst other achievements, was the inventor of natural-sounding dialogue in modern fiction. Tarantino's characters ramble on about pop music, Hemingway's about boxing or bullfighting.

Run-on or not, movie dialogue is like music. You either have an ear for it or you don't. Tin-eared dialogue is the deadly mark of the beginner. A writer whose dialogue sounds tinny is like a singer who can't carry a tune.

When they hear clunky dialogue, the producers in the audition seats just say, "Next."

Strong movie dialogue has a beat, a rhythm, and a melody. It is short and spare. It's an exchange of energy and bounces back and forth like a tennis ball – a punchy line followed by a comeback. The content can be sexual, physical, ideological or social. There is always conflict. Generally, no character speaks more than two or three lines. There should be no more than 10 words in a sentence. The more colloquial and natural the exchange, the better.

Consequently, the screenwriter has a professional interest in how English is spoken – right now – and he better have Big Ears. It's good to keep tabs on current slang, how the various age groups talk, and so on. Real people converse in sentence fragments, they shatter grammar, they hem and haw. Unless your character is a priss, making them talk in perfect sentences just creates bad dialogue. In a sense, screenwriting is method acting on the page. You have to become the character when you're writing their lines. A gift for mimicry doesn't hurt at all.

For example, in the Coen Brothers' film, *Burn After Reading*, Osbourne Cox, a self-deceiving upper-class twit, has been fired from his job at the CIA. He's discussing the matter with his wife, Katie, a pediatrician and champion bitch who just happens to be cheating on him.

A dialogue scene should have a single matter at issue between the characters. Here, it's the fact that Osbourne has been fired from his job. The scene begins with Katie's asking, "You quit?" The audience already knows that he's been fired; the point is that he's lying to his wife – and himself. When Osbourne tells Kate that he tried to tell her several times that he's left his job, this demonstrates that Katie no longer listens to anything her husband has to say. Then Katie says, "You *tried*? You *tried*? And then what, the aphasia kicked in?"

It's the clinical jargon of the "aphasia" line that gets the laugh and gives the scene punch.

Good dialogue like this resembles poetry. Every word counts. The order in which the words appear counts, too. In fiction, dialogue only has to play to the reader's inner ear, which is comparatively forgiving. In a film, actors say it aloud and that's a very different thing. If you read your dialogue audibly and it sounds awkward to your own ears, rewrite, rewrite.

Another good way of determining whether dialogue works is to remove the character names from the page and let the lines stand alone. If you can tell, without the characters being named, that it's two different people speaking, with separate attitudes, you have succeeded.

Occasionally, you may give a character a monologue, like Tarantino does in *True Romance,* where his hero, Clarence, does a funny riff on the subject of Elvis Presley, a very funny monologue worthy of a great stand-up comic. In his early films, Tarantino has a kind of fast-food aesthetic. Just as everybody in the audience has been to high school, they all know who Elvis is; the screenwriter is launched upon a topic he knows he and the audience have in common.

Monologues of a more sober nature can also resemble political or courtroom oratory. Sometimes they are, in fact, courtroom oratory. Here is an example from Michael Mann's film about John Dillinger, *Public Enemies,* written by Ronan Bennett. Dillinger's sleazy lawyer, Louis Piquett, is attempting to get the outlaw's place of incarceration moved out of Indiana, where the chances of escape are slight. Piquett's dialogue is intentionally fustian, an old-fashioned bit of courtroom table pounding. The very air of the courtroom, he claims, "reeks with the bloody rancor of intolerant malice."

And he demands that Dillinger's shackles be removed "forth-with."

Occasionally, movie dialogue resembles grand opera and employs not only arias and duets, but also trios. In *Sweet Smell of Success,* as its director, Alexander Mackendrick, points out, Clifford Odets occasionally triangulates his dialogue, bounces it between three characters rather than the standard duo, thus making it more persuasive.

Odets, the golden boy of 1930s class-conscious proletarian theater, wrote dialogue as a highly self-conscious hard-boiled street poetry. In one scene a shady press agent, Sidney Falco, played by Tony Curtis, is being harassed by an unhappy client, a bandleader named Jimmy Weldon.

Odets plays the conflict between Sidney and Weldon against the girl. Just as the dialogue of *Public Enemies* captures the rhetoric of a Midwest courtroom of the 1930s, Sidney's wisecracks fairly reek of raffish Broadway in the 1950s. Weldon says to his girl, "Joan, call a cop! We'll arrest this kid for larceny."

Once again, there's a single point at issue: Sidney's lack of PR results for Weldon. Information about him, such as the fact his fee is a hundred a week, is delivered by misdirection, not on the nose.

On-the-nose dialogue is guaranteed to clang and is the defining mark of the beginning screenwriter. The writer's atti-tude to OTN dialogue should be that of a surgeon towards a tumour. Another good example of how to avoid OTN dialogue is to be found in Nancy Meyers' *Something's Gotta Give.*

In a scene with the character's sister, Zoe, Meyers needs to impart the information that Erica, played by Diane Keaton, is divorced. If she just comes out and flat says it, she's writing on the nose. So, Meyers uses misdirection by sliding the scene's focus to the age of Erica's grown daughter, Marin. Zoe says that Marin was 23, old enough not to feel abandoned. How she felt, is not the point: by means of misdirection, Meyers has communicated the information that Erica is divorced

Meyers also employs colloquial word order in this scene. The character does not ask, "How old was Marin?" but "Marin was how old?" Also, Meyer elides Erica's response. The stilted version would read, "It was five years ago, she was 23." People, however don't talk like that, except in period films. Natural-sounding, conversational speech often turns sentences around backwards. So, we have the fragment, "Five years ago, so… 23." The viewer can sense Erica doing the math; the scene then becomes more persuasive.

Another way to avoid on-the-nose dialogue, as in any other form of prose, is to make adroit use of metaphor. Extended metaphor can be famously found in the dialogue of *The Big Sleep,* in the scene where Bogart and Bacall trade the euphemisms required by the Production Code of the era, when they talk flirty and dirty about "riding the horse" and "in the saddle."

Just as it does in poetry, metaphor enlivens dialogue. A person can be a "package," and a stripper can be "a tower of luscious legs."

As in everything else, however, character leads. If you want to write funny dialogue, make certain your protagonist is a funny person, given to quips or, at least, the sort of person that funny things happen to. If you don't have a sense of humour, don't try to write comedy.

In any event, your protagonist should be the driving force in every dialogue exchange, pushing the action. Since you want an A-list actor to be playing your character, give him the best lines. Don't waste the *bon mots* on a second banana or a day player. You should also give your lead character the *most* lines and thus the most screen time. The importance of a part is measured by the number of lines a character has to speak. In order to attract an A-list actor, put him on screen constantly.

An ambitious actor is looking for individual moments to shine; where he gets to do or say something unusual that will provide award fodder. While this was not my intention in creating the character of Jack Abramoff in *Casino Jack,* the role did garner a Golden Globe nomination for Kevin Spacey. All I wanted to do was capture the essence of a D.C. hustler. It was just my good fortune that this type of character is just the sort of anti-hero that Spacey enjoys playing.

Key to writing character-driven dialogue is the ability to hear a character's voice in your mind before committing it to the page. Think what friends or relatives the character might resemble. Recall the sound of their voice, their speech patterns before committing even one line to the page.

Most of all, remember you're telling a story in pictures. Dialogue is the icing on the cake, the froth on the surface. If you're all-consumed by dialogue, write a play.

Dialogue, most of all, and action, which we will discuss later, are the most important components of any individual scene in a screenplay. Description is less important, but any decent script must take it into consideration.

Description of setting and location creates the period and mood of a film. Location is the background against which the writer's characters play out their destiny. Some writers believe that the description details of landscape and cityscape are superfluous, unnecessary decoration.

But think how much the fog, the cobblestone streets, the gas lamps, contribute to, say, a movie about Sherlock Holmes. Unless the details of background are fully created, the characters themselves will lack conviction.

Film scenes are divided into exteriors and interiors. The novice screenwriter should keep in mind that it is cheaper to film interiors than exteriors. Period is expensive. The more exteriors, the bigger the budget. The more scenes there are, ditto. Long scenes may be slow. They are also cheaper. The bigger the budget, the less chance a rookie effort at screenwriting has of being produced.

Setting creates the arena in which the characters contest their will. In Hollywood films, New York and Los Angeles have made countless appearances. So much so, that there is now a staleness about them. For that very reason, Boston and Chicago have been lately pressed into service as fresher, and somehow more authentic. In Canadian films and television, the regions, the prairies especially, are deemed to be more authentic than the fleshpots of Toronto.

Where a novelist might spend many paragraphs to describe a city setting, the screenwriter, when introducing a character, should be brief.

Usually a single, symbolic image will suffice. Manhattan has been introduced too many times by its skyline. One shot of yellow taxis swarming in a sea of traffic will put your film's location across. The Hollywood sign has been used once too often to denote Los Angeles. Palm trees against a golden sunset are better, or even ocean surf pounding against rocks.

The conventional method of introducing a small town is a close shot of the highway sign bearing the town's name. White picket fences still do yeoman service to indicate to an audience a smaller location, with allegedly wholesome values.

A cornfield will nicely specify a rural locale. Lush green slopes are enough to describe the highlands of Colombia. Gothic churches and cobblestone streets say Europe. Onion domes say Russia.

Description of weather, too, has its uses to symbolize a setting. Rain usually means Great Britain, snow means Chicago or Minnesota. Sunshine usually signifies cheerful southern climes anywhere.

Period is more difficult to show and is by-and-large out of the writer's purview. It's pointless to spend a lot of time describing costume and decor, unless, of course, one fashion item symbolizes the era entirely.

You can give your character a fedora or a Stetson to indicate period. If he's driving an Auburn Speedster or a Hispano-Suiza, it's a good bet your film is taking place in the '20s or '30s, unless you mean him to be a vintage auto enthusiast.

The best way to portray period is through the popular culture of the time. Putting pop songs, radio and TV shows in the movie's background are a quick, efficient way of showing the era in which the story takes place. Even better is period dialogue. Learn how people spoke in the era you wish to depict. Nothing is worse than period films where historical characters talk like contemporaries.

Pop culture can also be good shorthand for describing character. If your protagonist watches daytime soaps, she's a low-rent person. If she listens to grand opera, she's aspiring to the upscale. If she's watching *I Love Lucy* reruns, she's stuck in the '50s or maybe just trying to live back in time.

Surroundings likewise help define character. A messy apartment, dishes piled up in the sink, and a couple of empty wine bottles lying around, help show a life in disarray, without the writer needing to use a line of dialogue.

In *The Assassination of Jesse James by the Coward Robert Ford*, when Jesse James, played by Brad Pitt, is described as living in a Kansas City cottage with a lawn plagued by weeds and a dying elm, we know that Jesse too is on the downswing. Like his rented house, he too has seen better days.

Conversely, a circular driveway with BMWs and Mercedes parked there are all that's necessary to indicate the surroundings of a successful, prosperous person.

(Oddly enough, it was that small cozy house with the white picket fence that showed American normality in past decades. Nowadays, it's the pseudo-colonial McMansion in the suburbs with the central hallway that serves as the film domicile of strong, normal families.)

There are screenwriters who believe that the less description you include in a script, the better. Others, certain that their work is going into production, don't even bother with it. They believe that the director's choice of location will settle all such matters.

For my part, I believe description of setting creates the mood and atmosphere that is one of the prime pleasures of film, and that it is up to the screenwriter to help create that mood.

In Robert Bolt's description of the Arabian desert in the classic *Lawrence of Arabia*, where he eloquently describes night in the desert, then the coming day of the leisurely shifting sands. Then, a rider, a small dot, appears on the horizon.

To my mind, that's film writing at its best.

BETWEEN
GOOD AND EVIL:
WRITING MORALITY

SAM GOLDWYN REPORTEDLY SAID, "If you want to send a message, try Western Union." He was probably thinking of the left progressive writers of his day, eager to uplift the Common Man through the movies Goldwyn was paying for.

But Goldwyn was wrong. Every film, even a Disney animated movie, sends a message of some sort. The screenwriter should at the very least be aware of the values and morals he's transmitting in his scripts, even if they are of the most conventional sort. After all, he's responsible for putting them there in the first place.

Therefore, the aspiring writer can create vivid character and place it in a well-defined dramatic structure but if he fails to create a moral universe that strikes a chord with the viewer, he will have failed.

Seeing is believing, as the critic Peter Biskind argues in his book of the same name. Film is so powerful a medium that a skilled filmmaker seems to be showing life as it's lived. Yes, viewers say, life happens just like that.

It's not just that, like it or not, every story has a moral, every story, every scene, every character has a moral component. The writer must always be aware of what he is saying about good and evil with his characters and situations.

Film, in a confluence of intricate energies, both reflects and creates reality; movies are fantasies that play a large part in people's lives, as propagandists from Josef Goebbels on down have not been slow to recognize. It is a powerful medium for persuasion; it influences how people behave, how they dress, what they buy, and most importantly, how they live their lives.

In the United States, the power of movies to influence behavior was remarked upon as early as the '30s. Before the institution of the Motion Picture Production Code of 1934, Hollywood films were quite different. Movies such as *Scarface* and *Blonde Crazy* frequently showed infidelity, homosexuality, brutal violence, and drug addiction. Shady characters were seen to profit from their deeds; attractive, willful women made opportunistic use of their sexuality to rise in the world. Gangsters frequently prospered; their violent actions regularly went unpunished. The screenwriters who wrote these films had no fancy notions about Truth in Art. Often ex-newspapermen, their instincts were rooted in tabloid sensationalism.

Seen today, these films, often starring James Cagney or Jean Harlow, are remarkable for their sense of authenticity. Pre-Code Hollywood films give the present-day viewer a better sense of what life actually looked like in the '30s than most of the era's works of serious art or literature.

Hollywood, from its inception, has always been seen by the great American hinterland as a Babylon-by-the-Pacific, a sink of immorality. The Hays Code, imposed in large part by the Catholic Church, sought to ameliorate the awful moral effects of Hollywood films, especially on children.

After the Code was enforced, drug addiction or homosexuality could not be portrayed in movies; sex outside marriage was shown as uniformly bad. No character would now profit from an evil deed. Now, all authority was to be respected. Films became God-fearing and patriotic. The moral regime enforced by the Hays Code was censorship at its worst. The sense of authenticity we now see in the early talkies was lost and films came to resemble fairy tales for adults.

The Hays Code had its desired effect. With a few honorable exceptions like *The Grapes of Wrath,* American movies pretty much ignored the Great Depression. Busby Berkeley musicals and costume dramas provided escapism for the unemployed masses. In those hard times, business was never better – for the movies. Of course, many of the writers of those escapist fantasies, a tidy irony, were communists.

World War II saw Hollywood produce blatant propaganda films on behalf of the patriotic war effort, as did the Cold War of the '50s. It was only in genre films, usually thought to be beneath serious notice, that subversive messages were occasionally smuggled through. Low-budget horror films, like *Invasion of the Body Snatchers*, were cinematic allegories attacking suburban conformity. Crime films like *The Asphalt Jungle* exposed urban corruption. Even children's films like *Black Beauty* campaigned on behalf of animal rights.

By the late '50s, the Hays Code had largely become a dead letter. Kennedy-era reformism saw a number of crusading films on subjects such as prison reform (*The Defiant Ones*), alcoholism (*Days of Wine and Roses*) and the evils of war (*Paths of Glory*).

All the same, the studios had internalized the moral conventions of the Hays Code and most Hollywood films obeyed a rigid morality. This attitude, of course, had changed by the late '60s. *Easy Rider* portrayed a couple of drug dealers as its heroes, even if Hopper and Fonda had to kill them off by the end. *Dr. Strangelove* roasted all authority with abandon, as did *One Flew Over the Cuckoo's Nest*. Sam Peckinpah celebrated violence in poetic slow motion. Unmarried sex went everywhere unpunished. Then, by the mid-'70s, the spirit of the Hays Code returned, if not the letter, in the blockbusters that followed the success of family-oriented films like *Star Wars*.

Now, as then, if a celebrity performs an action in a movie, that act must be worth emulating. I was once talking to a young woman in her 20s who was having a child. I asked her why.

She said, "Because all the movie stars are having babies."

We now have product placement for motherhood. In the past, movie stars, like Elizabeth Taylor, had many husbands as proof of her beauty. Now, like Angelina Jolie, they have many children, as a proof of virtue, even if these heroic mothers don't go through the inconvenience of actually giving birth.

The drama of motherhood has become a staple of current movies. Giving birth is seen as a kind of transcendent achievement for a woman. In these films, the climactic scene is one where the heroine is rushed to the hospital and ecstatically gives birth, an act previously so ordinary, it hardly seemed worth showing onscreen.

In the '50s, moms were played by the wholesome but dowdy June Allyson. Dad was pipe-smoking Robert Young. Now, mom is Britney Spears and dad is Brad Pitt. In the '40s and '50s, the hero portrayed by Humphrey Bogart or John Wayne was a man alone. He was never anybody's father.

Actors you would want to attract to your script are often extremely conscious about the moral and political actions of the characters you would have them play. I once wrote a movie that starred a certain African-American leading man. Let's call him Sonny Jones, since that was the alias he used at his hotel to discourage the nonexistent hordes of his fans.

I hadn't written the part for a black man, but the exigencies of casting prevailed, as well as the fact that the producer wanted to do the dude a favor, yadda, yadda, yadda. Matters were not helped along by the fact that he was completely dominating the film's director. He swallowed the guy, as Vinny Lawrence would say, with a glass of water.

Often, a screenwriter serves as an ambassador on a film set, performing shuttle diplomacy between producers, director, and actors. I was dispatched to Sonny's hotel room to make adjustments to my script.

Sonny had us in an awkward position. He knew that our film was only going into production because of his participation. As he chatted with his wife back home in California, his assistant/girlfriend perched nearby. Soon, they would be negotiating a threesome with the PR chick. The movie itself happened to be a crime drama in which the hero had to choose between two women. Sonny saw his character as just another promiscuous black man; he asked me to change the role. Despite the blatant hypocrisy, Sonny wanted to be a good example to his people.

Sometimes, screenwriters aren't that different from the women who do wardrobe and makeup. I did my best to oblige. The resulting film is best forgotten.

Sonny Jones was a rarity in that he was frank about his ideological interests. Most often, ideology comes from producers and executives in the guise of market decisions – what will sell with the audience, and what won't. Hollywood and Washington ask the same question: "Will it play in Peoria?" Politicians, like filmmakers, are always asking themselves, "What's the narrative?" (In the 2008 Democratic primaries, Hillary Clinton provided the American public with a movie moment: she learned how to cry.) Like the political propagandist, it is the job of the screenwriter to take the pulse of the audience, weekly, perhaps daily, and adjust accordingly.

Together with schools and the other media, as the Hays Code recognized, movies create social values, sometimes not the most desirable ones. For instance, in 1919, with its positive portrayal of lynching, D.W. Griffith's racist *Birth of a Nation* helped give the Ku Klux Klan a second wind in America, even bringing it into the cities of the North, where it had never before had a foothold.

In 1972, *The Godfather*, on a slightly more positive note, helped create the family values that have been prevalent for the last 40 years.

Write it and it happens.

Disillusion with society, government, and the legitimate authorities at the time of Vietnam and Watergate in the mid-'70s, when *The Godfather* was released, made "The Family" seem honorable in comparison. Where gangsters, like Jimmy Cagney in *White Heat,* had previously been portrayed as thugs and sickos, Francis Ford Coppola made the Corleones seem warm, powerful ethnics, a noble source of justice and especially honor. Coppola accomplished this transvaluation of values by making all the other gangsters, the corrupt cops and politicians that he portrayed in the film *much worse than the mobsters.*

The way *The Godfather* showed it, the average American was in the exact same position as a Sicilian peasant centuries ago: you could only get justice from the "family," since you couldn't obtain it from government or legitimate society. Coppola's moral stance, pointing out the religious hypocrisy of the Corleone family, was pure '60s counterculture, but the sheer glamour he achieved in their portrayal pointed viewers in quite the opposite ideological direction. The *Godfather* films reaffirmed traditional social values by giving them the glamour of rebellion associated with Marlon Brando since *The Wild One.* Moreover, *The Godfather: Part II* is the favorite movie of all studio executives since it mostly consists of business meetings punctuated by killings.

Peter Biskind demonstrates that dysfunctional families populated the films of the '50s, such as *Rebel Without a Cause,* with many weak fathers and domineering mothers. In this, Nicholas Ray's most famous film, James Dean's dad wears a kitchen apron, so the movie can show just how emasculated he's become. In the present era, post-women's liberation, that same kitchen apron would probably mean that Jimmy's dad was a supremely enlightened man.

But, in *The Godfather*, Marlon Brando is not at all a dickless dad; he is a feudal lord with the power of life and death, and the moral arbiter of how a father behaves with his family.

Weddings are key to how a movie treats the entire subject of family. If, as in *The Godfather*, a wedding is depicted as a warm, wonderful celebration, then the film celebrates the institution of the family. If the wedding is shown as a ridiculous farce, as in *Rachel Getting Married*, or *The Graduate*, then a more critical view of the family is on the screen.

Since *The Godfather*, the writer must think hard about his feeling about the institution of the family.

How do you write a family that a viewer will admire?

First of all, you write a young family. In the family of the American Dream, mom and dad are just the oldest kids. The kids themselves are pre-teens; mom and dad have torrid sex constantly. Everybody plays sports together, sports being the other American religion. Dad, above all, is the Father of a Shortstop.

However, families are, on occasion, portrayed negatively in American films. This negative depiction occurs in movies like *Knocked Up* and *Juno* when a couple stays in a bad marriage. Their sin? The marriage is dead but husband and wife fail to realize it's time to move onto the next spouse.

Hollywood films may believe in family. They also believe firmly in divorce.

Good and bad movie characters can be quickly defined by their relationships with children. A bad father doesn't show up for his kids' little league baseball game or school play. A bad mom ignores the kiddies to go out on dates. Either these reprobates mend their ways by Act Three or you punish them severely, possibly by death. If your movie appears to condone lousy parenting, the audience will hate you and your film.

The rise of family as subject matter for film has a very practical basis. It is roughly contemporary with the globalization of film. Politics and sports, as well as many other subjects, are local and don't travel well. However, everybody on the planet who goes to the movies understands love, sex, children and family.

Biskind argues that a film's character arc usually signals a film's political beliefs. If a soft male learns to be hard, as in *Straw Dogs*, then the conservative lesson is clear. If a tough guy learns to be sensitive, as Jon Voigt does in *Coming Home*, then the opposing belief system is being espoused. If a city is portrayed as an urban jungle, then you're presenting a case for Social Darwinism. If your bad guys triumph over the protagonist, you're making a statement about the world that he – and the audience – live in.

Films with a conservative political stance prefer force to persuasion. *Dirty Harry* is the best example. In liberal films, cops are often seen as bigots and bullies. If a film depicts a terrorist as a radical environmentalist, you pretty much know what its politics are.

Conservative can be differentiated from liberal, according to Biskind, by their attitude to the People, especially in westerns. If they're good decent townspeople, the film has a liberal slant. If they're a mob crazed by greed, it's conservative.

The same goes for a film's attitude to the media. If, as in *All the President's Men*, the protagonists are two crusading, heroic reporters, it's liberal. If it's *Absence of Malice*, where a sensation-seeking press falsely maligns a good decent business guy, the opposite holds true.

Even if a film is a popcorn movie, a silly comedy or non-stop action-adventure film, with no ambitions whatever, it still has an ideology and a morality. That is to say, if a movie is deliberately inoffensive, by its very lack of morality, it endorses the status quo. Happy endings, as Biskind says, are essentially optimistic. They reflect the belief that life is essentially good in the society they inhabit. It flatters the audience who lives in it happily.

The film industry itself, however, is neither moral nor immoral; it is amoral. It will make films to suit any morality for which it believes there's an audience. Hollywood can make a film about Che Guevara as easily as it makes a film about Jesus Christ. It would make Muslim fundamentalist films if it thought American viewers would pay to watch them.

If you make one group of people the protagonists and another the antagonists, you are endorsing the former. You can take any group whatsoever, Nazis, for example, and show them as principled and courageous, and you have endorsed their ideology.

It's instructive to note how filmmakers have of late attempted to sentimentalize harsh and domineering characters such as J. Edgar Hoover and Margaret Thatcher, turning them into sympathetic protagonists by portraying them as underdogs, Hoover as a gay, Thatcher as addled, a shattered survivor of politics. These films purposely omit little details like Hoover's part in the red hunts of the '50s or Thatcher's suppression of the striking British miners. Both these films enjoyed limited success with audiences, proof that the attempt to portray Hoover and Thatcher as underdogs was less than a triumph.

(Both biopics tell a historical story by focusing on their subject's personal and family lives, soap-opera style. By these lights, you could write Napoleon's life story in film by zeroing in on marriage and divorce from Josephine, emphasizing the Emperor's desire for a son and heir. You could omit the Battle of Waterloo and the Retreat from Moscow as merely boring, unless they caused him to miss the school play.)

At the present time, minorities – Native people, African Americans, and gays – are always good. You can't have a minority villain without balancing matters out with a good guy member of the same group. Otherwise, you leave yourself open to charges of racism.

If a drug dealer is a member of a minority, as in *American Gangster*, it's okay to go ahead and make him into a hero. Ditto, if he's good to his mom and dad, as in *Blow*. If he's the protagonist of a stoner comedy, like *Pineapple Express,* that's okay too, if he's just selling grass.

Otherwise, better kill him off by the end of Act Two.

In movies, good and bad are delineated by actions. Bad guys have annoying habits, they chew gum noisily, they have colds, and they are overweight. Good guys are mild and reasonable.

In film, who dies and why says where the movie stands morally. The manner in which a film rewards and punishes its characters says where it stands as well.

In *Training Day*, for instance, the corrupt cop, played by Denzel Washington, is blown away in the last five minutes. Jake Hoyt, the rookie, goes home to his wife. In the theatrical version, the stolen drug money ends up in the police evidence room. In the DVD version, the cash ends up in Jake's pocket. I suppose the audience is considered more tolerant while in their own homes.

As Biskind says, a film's final speaker always articulates its essential moral lesson. For instance, in *Sweet Smell of Success,*

J.J. Hunsecker, played by Burt Lancaster is a powerful red-baiting newspaper columnist, a Bill O'Reilly of the print era. His final speech articulates very well how the 1930s progressive Clifford Odets felt about the arrogance and power of the opinion makers of his time, as he pillories the majority of humanity as midgets and pygmies. "Only a great person understands another great person," he says. "And that leaves you out."

When a film like *Sweet Smell of Success* punishes a false achievement like Hunsecker's, the convention is that the script uses his family life to do it. The final speech is given when his niece, the only person close to him, leaves him in disgust at his attempts to control her life. When a character is seen to have achieved success by ruthless or evil means, the screenwriter always punishes him via his family. A child's death is often used to punish a character's bad behavior.

In *There Will Be Blood,* Paul Thomas Anderson's adaptation of Upton Sinclair's *Oil!,* Daniel Day-Lewis's prospector, Daniel Plainview, ruthlessly carves out a fortune through sharp business practices. The film punishes him when his adopted son, H.W., is deafened, through his negligence, in an oil rig explosion. The notion is that Plainview has sacrificed what's most dear to him for money. All the same, American films, unlike Greek drama are reluctant to depict the family, as an institution, as an arena for tragedy.

The worst villain in movies is the person that harms a child. You can torture, maim, and otherwise mutilate a child molester.

The audience won't mind.

The best example of this phenomenon is *Man on Fire,* also starring Denzel Washington, this time as a good guy, a bodyguard hired to protect a young girl in Mexico City. When a gang of kidnappers attempt to abduct his young charge, the bodyguard captures one of them, cuts off his ear, his fingers, and duct tapes the kidnapper to his car and sets them both on fire.

Only what the bastard deserved, am I right?

If somebody hurts his family in any way, the Father of a Shortstop has full permission to turn into a psycho killer. The stern father's revenge has become a sub-genre in itself in films like *Ransom*. No vengeance is too extreme against those who would threaten a man's family.

In a similar vein, the villains of *The Girl with the Dragon Tattoo* are Swedish Nazis and sexual abusers of women. You would think it would be open season on guys like that. Any agonizing torture the writer might devise should be heartily approved by the audience.

Not so.

When Lisbeth Salander gets the chief abuser in her sights, the evil Swede obligingly crashes his Volvo and blows himself up. This particular story beat is the acme of cinematic political correctness. To the mind of a studio exec, even dispatching a Nazi abuser of women might render a movie's protagonist less than sympathetic to the segment of the audience who disapproves of violence.

In the same vein, Steve Zaillian sets up the sex scene between Lisbeth Salander and Mikael Blomkvist by first having the movie's anti-masculinist hero take a bullet from the Swedish Nazis, thus rendering him wounded, vulnerable and thus *deserving* of womanly succor and sexual healing.

In our times, a man alone is not a hero.

Most likely, he's a serial killer.

A typical serial killer lives alone in a low-rent apartment, surrounded by stacks of old newspapers. He scribbles endlessly in his journals, a sure sign of dangerous eccentricity.

In general, the screenwriter must set up the major events in his story in a manner that satisfies morality. One of the best examples is Hitchcock's classic, *Psycho*. It's extremely important that Janet Leigh be established as an immoral woman before Anthony Perkins, in drag, carves her up in the shower.

Not only does Janet, a woman alone, have adulterous sex, she also embezzles money from her boss. If poor Janet was say, a wonderful mom going to visit a sick aunt, the audience of the time would have been outraged at what befalls her at the Bates Motel.

A similar morality is at work in any slasher movie. In this puritanical society, sexual revolution or no, sex is still seen as sinful. It's crucial, then, that the women slasher victims are shown as sexually active before they too get it in the neck.

If one of your characters is married, or even has a steady girlfriend, you must never show him having sex with anybody else. If he does, he's a monster. If, on the other hand, his wife or girlfriend is unfaithful, well then, that justifies anything he might do with another woman.

In *American Beauty*, for instance, the character played by Annette Bening, Carolyn Burnham, is not only an unfaithful wife to Kevin Spacey, she also cuts down a tree. Cutting down a tree is almost worse than kicking a dog. After a character cuts down a tree, anything a writer might do to her is well deserved. She's now fair game.

(Catastrophe, by the way, is always a good way to start a movie, a wonderful inciting incident. Give your character a cheating wife, misbehaving children, trouble at the office, and the rest of the film almost writes itself. Happiness, as Martin Amis is fond of saying, writes white on the page.)

Sex, of course, is hedged around with many taboos in the movies. Biskin recounts how Marilyn Monroe, in the '50s, was always presented as a dumb blonde, when in real life she was anything but stupid. It was felt that Monroe's bombshell sexuality, combined with brains, would be just too intimidating for the average male viewer.

In a similar vein, Marlon Brando, in his films of the same era, was beaten up, repeatedly. There was a general feeling that his rebellious sexuality, which was at the heart of his appeal, had to be controlled and punished in some way. The notion that such animal vigor existed somewhere, free and at large, was also too much for the audience of the time.

Women in film are often the custodians of values. In the late '40s, the *femme fatale* of the crime films of the era, conflated sexuality with death and danger. In the classic western, the schoolteacher in the gingham frock sets the hero straight and sets him firmly on his course of virtuous action.

That was then. In the present era of serial monogamy, the audience is so confused and mistrustful of relationships with the opposite sex, that the custodian of values is often an older person, often belonging to a minority group – or even a child.

Relationships are so morally explosive at this point that films often avoid portraying a love interest. In this instance, it's instructive to compare Steve Zaillian's early draft of *Moneyball* with the completed film. In the course of rebuilding the Oakland A's via statistics, the script's hero, Billy Beane, is established as divorced.

As a divorced man, he has on-again, off-again girlfriends, occasional one-night stands – the usual bachelor conduct. This behavior, apparently, was deemed "unsympathetic" by the studio because, in the final film, Beane's sole relationship is with his young daughter. Any sexual relationship outside of marriage is becoming strongly taboo in a film that aspires to a general audience, *just as in the days of the Hays Code.*

There are religious groups out there that may conceivably be offended by free and easy sexuality, and a studio film does not want to risk losing one potential audience member.

Even in matters less salient than sexual behavior, the viewer must feel that good fortune or bad is deserved. If something bad is about to befall a character, then you often prepare the audience by having the character do a minor kindness. Old people are helpful in this regard. Conversely, if misfortune is about to occur, have them be rude to a waiter or something of the sort. In either case, the audience will feel they have it, good or bad, coming to them.

Finally, the writer can deal with morality by undercutting it entirely. David Webb Peoples did this brilliantly in Clint Eastwood's revisionist western, *Unforgiven.* His character, the outlaw William Munny, at the end of the story, even though he's a good dad, sticks a shotgun in brutal town marshal Little Bill's face. Little Bill says, "I don't deserve this...to die like this. I was building a house." Replies Munny, "'Deserve' has nothing to do with it." Then, he pulls the trigger.

This one scene negates the morality of the hundreds of westerns that came before. It also has the unmistakable ring of truth.

Ultimately, a screenwriter is like a lawyer or a political speechwriter; he should be able to make a case for any ideological position. At the same time, as well as being good and bad films, there are two further categories: movies you like and movies you don't like. It's hard to keep self-respect if you work on too many film or television projects whose ideological message you don't like.

Writerly conscience is one thing: knowing how to articulate a moral or political position in visual storytelling is another. If you change your own values too many times to suit networks and studios, just to keep working, you end up a hack and a cynic. Worse, you no longer know what you believe yourself. All the luxury cars and houses in the world won't make up for that.

Pangs of conscience, I believe, are behind much celebrity activism. Self-disgust at taking too many roles that they don't believe in, in the interest of a large paycheque, results in self-imposed penance in the slums of Haiti and amongst African orphans.

In my opinion, it's easier to work on films in which you believe.

THE LANGUAGE
OF ACTION:
WRITING VIOLENCE

A DISCUSSION OF THE PORTRAYAL of sex and violence in films is
not a simple matter. The supposed exploitation of these two
subjects serves as the excuse that social conservatives and pro-
gressives, both latter-day proponents of a new Hays Code, use
as their chief argument for censorship, or at least censure, of the
movies. Violence in films, they say, begets violence in life. The
benign portrayal of sexuality in film, similarly leads to promis-
cuity, teenage pregnancy and other social ills. Whether or not

there's any truth to this doubtful proposition, I leave to others. I only know that both subjects will continue to be treated in movies and that, as a professional screenwriter, you're expected to master them.

Let's examine the screenwriter's relation to violence in film.

First of all, the blood is only cornstarch with red dye, the bullets are not real, the wounds are just squibs.

It's only a movie.

But, from the beginning, violent action has been a part of motion pictures. Moving planes, trains, cars, boats, runners, fighters, car chases, crashes, explosions – anything in motion – looks good on the screen. Violence, too, is kinetic and goes with the movies like ham goes with eggs. If the aspiring scribe hankers to write contemporary thrillers, or science fiction, or horror films, learning how to write action sequences is inescapably part of the equation.

As the critic David Bordwell argues, extended physical action is a key component of the blockbuster cinema of the past few decades. Where directors like Spielberg and Lucas have showcased spectacle and screen energy, an "impact esthetic" has ruled. Movies now routinely depict continuous physical action, occasionally interrupted by a dialogue scene.

Even so, writing persuasive action sequences is also an extension of character development. Action results from character. Unless the film is broad farce, you don't expect to see a comic character in a gun battle, immersed in a world of deadly force, any more than you expect to see a romantic lead, such as Hugh Grant, duking it out in a bar brawl. Consequently, even when he's wielding a machine gun, a film persona's actions must be an extension of his character and personality.

Action divorced from character is mechanical, rather like sex without love. Fundamentally, violent action is best conceptualized as emotional conflict between characters – plus a weapon. The writer can blow up everything in sight, crash a hundred vehicles, and still bore the audience. The large number of action movies that bomb at the box office or go straight to video prove that, unless action comes out of compelling character, audiences will yawn.

Action characters, both male and female, have much in common with dancers and athletes. It's a pleasure to watch John Wayne or Clint Eastwood, when they're playing gunslingers, move on screen. Lee Marvin's physical movements, weapon in hand, are as elegant as any soft-shoe by Fred Astaire.

Whether or not played by Marvin or Wayne, or somebody else, American movies portray violence by developing the character of the gunslinger. Although he has taken various forms over time, as Neill Hicks suggests, the character essentially remains the same down through the years. Before attempting to write this gunman character, it's worth tracing his history:

The roots of the action character go back to the dime novels of the 19th century. Even before he was wielding a firearm, this action character was prominent in Sir Walter Scott's novels about Scottish border reivers, armed with sabres and rapiers. The Code of the West is identical to the Code of the Borders, transported to the American frontier via the Deep South, where Scott's novels were read with fascination. (Violence, it seems, is a matter of social structure. Anthropologists tell us that wherever you have societies based on cattle, you have rustlers, range wars, and violence. Nowadays, this violent Code of Respect is most alive, thanks to the movies, not in cattle country, but in the black urban ghetto.)

The character of the cowboy gunfighter, then, defines right and wrong by violent action, just as he did when he herded cattle on the Scottish borders. Whether played by Henry Fonda or Brad Pitt, he is a man of Protestant principle and determination who can carve his way through life, beholden to no one and answerable only to God.

The gunslinger character has very little to do with the history of the frontier and everything to do with the mythmaking of the movie writers. The cowboy gunfighter can always mow down large numbers of the opposition without suffering a nick himself. He always comes out a winner in the end; when it comes down to a shootout, he is unbeatable.

The Man With No Name, the mythological gunfighter played by Clint Eastwood in Sergio Leone's spaghetti westerns is, in fact, the Angel of Death. He appears and punishes the wicked with gunfire, then vanishes. Anton Chigurh, in *No Country for Old Men*, although he is the antagonist, plays the identical character. Chigurh, yet another dream figure, is also the Angel of Death who comes to dispatch the righteous and sinners alike. He's still unbeatable. The hero of the movie, Tommy Lee Jones, throws in the towel on his entire career, rather than go up against him.

From Tom Mix to Clint Eastwood, the cowboy gunfighter is a a rural figure. In order to create dramatic tension, those writers who invent him create a city slicker from Back East, an Englishman or even a European, as his antagonist. The English villain, usually a powerful ranch owner, is a staple of westerns, even a neo-western such as *Unforgiven,* where Richard Harris plays a character named English Bob.

Neill Hicks discusses how, over time, the character of the cowboy gunslinger turns into the city gangster, trading in his

Colt for a Smith & Wesson and, more recently, a Glock. But, essentially, the gunslinger character remains the same, except that he is now a member of an ethnic minority – Irish, Italian, Jewish, Latino, Asian, or Black.

The cowboy gunfighter generally espouses law and order. For the most part, the gangster or city gunman scorns traditional morality in order to win wealth and power. Where the cowboy gunfighter wins the love of the town schoolteacher because of his moral righteousness, the gangster, instead, uses raw violence to secure the love of an upper-class girl.

Over time, the character of the gangster eventually evolves into the private detective. The private eye is still a gunman but, like the cowboy, he fights to uphold justice. For instance, Humphrey Bogart began his movie career portraying gangsters. He then became a cinematic legend in the role of Sam Spade, a character who inhabits a moral landscape halfway between cop and crook.

Unlike Bogart, Jimmy Cagney could never play a convincing cop of any stripe. For one thing, the actor who played psycho killer Cody Jarrett lacked Bogart's judiciousness. Cagney had too much Erin Isle belligerence to convince audiences that he was a seeker after law and order.

Over time, the private eye character, Hicks argues, such as the one played by Bogart, evolves into the rogue cop, also a gunslinger. The rogue cop, like the private eye, fights outside the rules to uphold justice. But he has a badge; behind him lies the authority of society. The cowboy actor Clint Eastwood, in *Dirty Harry*, plays the classic rogue cop. The rogue cop, of course, is the archetypal hero of a hundred television series and thousands of mystery novels. He is forever at odds with his superiors; he is forever going outside the rules to ensure his own, purer notion of justice, with his gun.

The rogue cop, in his turn, eventually evolves into the secret agent. Whether C.I.A. or MI5, the character now operates, not in the confines of the city, but in the international arena. He's still a gunslinger. From Richard Hannay of *The 39 Steps* to James Bond and George Smiley of *Tinker, Tailor, Soldier, Spy*, rather than uphold law and order, his aim is to save the Western World from destruction at the hands of its enemies.

Bond's creator, Ian Fleming, was strongly influenced by Raymond Chandler. Bond is Philip Marlowe let loose in the international arena, endowed by Fleming with tastes that are more sophisticated and with much better luck with women. Fleming also copied Chandler's typical inciting incident when he sends Bond into dangerous situations that have resulted in the death of the first agent who tackled it, just as Marlowe, in *The Big Sleep*, follows in the steps of Vivian Sternwood's missing husband, Rusty Regan.

The anomaly, the other side of the coin, is John le Carré's secret agent, George Smiley, in *Tinker Tailor Soldier Spy*. He is, of course, the anti-Bond, a small, dumpy bespectacled civil servant, whose wife cuckolds him with dismaying regularity, and whose main form of investigation takes place amongst files of documents. Smiley is most definitely not a gunslinger and never shoots anybody, never orders a martini, nor does he have sex. Nonetheless, he is the perfect British public school hero, decent, honorable, muddling through. Smiley is more like the viewer himself; James Bond is the man the viewer wishes he were.

Meanwhile, back at the ranch, the cowboy gunfighter evolves, in the spaghetti western, into the character of the bounty hunter. In his equivocal position between the law and personal vengeance, he is a more complex figure, more like a rural rogue cop. As portrayed by Eastwood in the films of Sergio Leone, he is a rogue lawman, amoral, feral, and surpassingly violent. Yet, the bounty hunter becomes a political revolutionary in spaghetti westerns like *A Fistful of Dynamite* and *A Bullet for the General*. And the super-violent spaghetti western, at this point, becomes a vehicle for the pop treatment of serious issues.

Meanwhile, government man James Bond evolves into Jason Bourne, the rogue agent of *The Bourne Identity*. Rather than save the Western World, he's using his gun to save his ass. Bourne's the hero of the age of mass paranoia: his own government is out to get him.

Denzel Washington's rogue agent becomes a bodyguard in *Man on Fire*. The gunman now doesn't defend an entire community as in the western. One child only is under his protection; one family alone represents the horizon of his concern. The atomization of the society from which the movie springs couldn't be clearer.

Then, in films like *Inglourious Basterds,* Quentin Tarantino transforms the gunman bounty hunter of the spaghetti westerns into a vengeful rogue commando leader played by Brad Pitt, in what can only be called *Once Upon a Time in the Holocaust*.

NOW, THINGS CHANGE IN A MAJOR WAY.

The gunslinger gives up his guns.

The martial arts fad that results from the influence of Hong Kong movies, combined with growing alarm over gun violence in American cities, makes the reputations of Jackie Chan and Bruce Lee and all their Caucasian followers. They are practitioners of violence whose firepower is in their fists. Their violence becomes balletic.

The advent of the superhero protagonist also contributes to the diminishing of gun violence in movies. Superman himself is so strong he has no need of a weapon. His ability to fly is superseded by the super powers of Spiderman, who can leap from building to building. In the era of CGI, Spidey's bouncing around the city skyline makes for far more spectacular visuals than a mere shootout or car chase. Spiderman, like most of his fans, is a geeky adolescent, making identification easier for teenagers.

Batman, like Superman, is an adult, but he has no superpowers, just extraordinary intellectual and physical abilities. It is pure characterization that makes him pre-eminent as a superhero. Since Batman's parents were murdered, this childhood trauma has transformed the superhero into a dark, brooding presence, given to prolonged sulks in the Batcave.

Unlike Superman, Batman is a Byronic romantic in a cape and tights. This is the secret of his lasting appeal. His lifelong quest for vengeance against criminals gives emotional impetus to all his many action sequences. Where Superman is Olympian, Batman is more human, is motivated by much more pain and anger.

Then, as our action man further evolves from the superhero, something else happens:

He turns into a woman.

Women action heroes, when they first appeared in the 1970s, were less than persuasive. The heroines of *Charlie's Angels* and films like *Foxy Brown* were sexy babes with .45s and karate kicks, as well as major T&A. The general effect was of girls wearing their boyfriends' fedoras.

Cute, but unconvincing.

The violence in these films starring women action heroes was out of character in terms of the gender of the protagonists. Mostly, the audience, especially women, failed to respond to them. Now, the films in which they appeared are mostly seen as camp oddities.

But the woman action hero was still evolving. The more androgynous character of Lisbeth Salander, of *The Girl with the Dragon Tattoo,* was more authentically female than the *Charlie's Angels*-style action hero in her attitude to violence. Her physical aggression consists of disarming violent males, by means of handcuffs and tasers, and rendering them harmless. The character played by Angelina Jolie in *Salt* is also somewhat androgynous. Like Jason Bourne, she is a rogue agent. Like Lisbeth Salander, her violence is mostly self-protective and defensive. In any event, Jason Bourne and Lisbeth Salander are the state-of-the-art action heroes. Any new action character the aspiring writer is thinking to create must take them as the point of departure.

WHETHER HIS PEOPLE ARE MALE or female, the writer who wishes to write convincing action sequences must, first of all, establish that the characters are living in a world of deadly force. The Coen Brothers, adapting Cormac McCarthy, do an exemplary job of establishing the right setting for action in the opening scene of *No Country for Old Men.* Llewelyn Moss, played by Josh Brolin, while out hunting along the Tex-Mex border, happens across a drug deal gone bad. He finds abandoned vehicles, bullet-riddled bodies of men and dogs, and two million dollars cash in an attaché case.

There's no mistaking the universe Brolin has entered: the viewer has now been set up to expect more violence and he gets it.

The character played by Brolin, Llewelyn Moss, is an experienced hunter, well versed in the use of firearms. Any man or woman of action, whether they are cowboy, cop, gangster, or spy, must have training of some kind, in order to be believable. They can't be a dentist or an accountant. They possess martial skills and strategic resources. In addition, they must possess a personal or professional code of honor that must be upheld regardless of cost. When the character lacks the skill set and the code, as does Russell Crowe's community-college teacher in Paul Haggis' *The Next Three Days,* it seems out of character, when he starts shooting it out with the bad guys. Where did he learn those moves?

Possibly in other Russell Crowe movies.

Unlike this community-college teacher, the hero of action must have a full grasp of what is required; he must be determined to see through to the end a fight of epic proportions.

In order for it to be dramatic, the action hero's task is always a Mission Impossible. He will always be overmatched. He must take immediate action. This holds true for the gangster as for the cop.

For instance, the key to the action sequences in Michael Mann's *Public Enemies* lies in the character of John Dillinger, as played by Johnny Depp. The essential core of his persona, and consequently the film's actions scenes as invented by Mann and his writers, is that Dillinger is willing to go toe-to-toe with the FBI in lethal combat.

Dillinger is certainly overmatched. Despite his courage and élan, there's no way he can beat the U.S. government. Dillinger's attitude to what amounts to a death sentence is a soldier's existentialism: "We don't worry about tomorrow," he says, "because we're having too good a time today."

In all his films, Mann is obsessed with the technical expertise of professionals. So, he gives us a scene in this film, unique in the genre, where Dillinger discusses the workings of his Thompson with the mob gunsmith who's supplying him, mentioning malfunctioning springs and Cutts compensators, in a showy display of technical expertise.

Only Michael Mann would mention the Cutts compensator, the Thompson's recoil brake. All the same, if you're going to depict weaponry in action, it doesn't hurt to research it in the interests of authenticity.

John Dillinger meets his match, not in Melvin Purvis but in Charles Winstead, the Texas lawman recruited by Hoover, who ultimately guns him down in front of the Biograph Theater. Their initial confrontation is an armed showdown during the siege of Little Bohemia. The action consists of a rapid unfolding of details of gunfighting virtuosity, as Dillinger and Winstead shoot on the run and Winstead even flips a somersault, Tommy in hand, and comes up firing.

Mann's details of the weaponry and ammunition – 10-gauge shotgun and the 5-shot bursts – help make the scene persuasive. What makes it remarkable is Mann's depiction of Agent Winstead's athletic ability to roll away from Dillinger's fire and reload simultaneously, an aspect of his character as a traditional cowboy gunfighter, even if he is working for the FBI.

To take another example, there's a scene in the Coen Brothers' *Fargo* that shows how much character enriches action.

A Minnesotan state trooper stops two bad guys, Carl Showalter and Gaear Grimsrud, when they're transporting Jean, a kidnap victim, in their car trunk. Showalter, a sleazebag played by Steve Buscemi, fails to bribe his way out of the situation. Grimsrud, a violent psychopath, reacts in character by brutally murdering the trooper to Buscemi's shock and amazement, grabbing him by the hair before he puts the pistol to his head.

As in *Fargo,* the violence in Dominik's film is more effective in the context of dramatic scene. Ed Miller is one of the James Gang, who's vainly trying to contain Jesse's violence in the course of a train robbery. The violence in the outlaw's character is revealed in a scene that combines action and dialogue. When the baggage master of the train they're robbing refuses to open a safe, Jesse smashes him on the head with his pistol and says, "They need the convincing. They got their company rules and I got my mean streak and that's how we get things done around here." When Miller begs him not to kill the baggage master, Jesse says, "Do not tell me what I can and cannot do, Ed."

Needless to say, Ed isn't much longer for this world. The quaint formality of Jesse's dialogue, by virtue of contrast, serves to emphasize his violence. If he were merely a dumb thug, the scene would be cliché. Jesse's down-home reasonableness serves to enhance the sense of evil.

MOVING TO SWORDPLAY FROM gunfighting, the aspiring screen-writer need look no further than to Ridley Scott's first feature, *The Duellists*, based on a Joseph Conrad short story. As far as I know, Scott's film, about a couple of feuding French hussars during the Napoleonic wars, has the only sword-fighting sequences that show what it is actually like to face five feet of razor-sharp steel. In this case, the truth of the duel is conveyed, not particularly by the writing but by the sound of steel on steel.

Finally, whether it's a crime film or a western, whether the characters are carrying swords or firearms, audiences do not wish to be subjected to the horrors of authentic violence. They don't want to know what it's like to actually get shot or stabbed. So, while Steven Spielberg can give viewers, in *Saving Private Ryan,* all the flying limbs and spilled intestines of the Normandy invasion, he can also, in *War Horse,* give them the entire Battle of the Somme without showing a single drop of blood. When it comes to writing violence, the writer must know just how much of it his audience can take.

LIKE VIOLENCE, SEX HAS ALWAYS been a staple of the movies. And like sex, the treatment of sex has evolved over the years. Still, it too consists of a number of conventions.

For decades, the close-up of the big romantic kiss was the signature image of the movies themselves. As for anything more than a kiss, Hollywood hastily moved past the actual lovemaking to the conversation afterwards, if not the cheerful – or otherwise – morning after.

Then, in the '50s, there was an entire sub-genre wherein Doris Day preserved her virtue from the rampaging male lust of Rock Hudson. In those days, in movies, married couples were obliged to sleep chastely in twin beds. Even by the mid-'70s, the Ontario censors were perturbed because a film I wrote – my first – contained a scene with the woman on top. Little did those good prudish Canadian gents know that by 2012, woman on top was almost obligatory for cinematic sex.

Sex meets violence in the genre of the erotic thriller. Consequently, films like *Basic Instinct, Sea of Love,* and *Eyes Wide Shut* represent a transitional genre that thrived mostly during the '80s and '90s. The genre's association of sex and death played well with audiences in the age of AIDS and accordingly served to set up the marriage-and-family-centered films of the present era.

In *Basic Instinct,* for example, Sharon Stone stabs a rock star to death with an ice pick during sex. In *Dressed to Kill,* Angie Dickinson picks up a stranger in an art gallery then has sex with him in a taxi. After she finds out the dude has an unpleasant social disease, she splits his apartment only to be slashed to death in the elevator. In *Sea of Love,* Al Pacino discovers that Ellen Barkin is not murdering those men who have the temerity to sleep with her, it's just her psycho ex-husband who's doing the knife work. (For some reason, razor-sharp blades feature heavily in erotic thrillers. I guess they're more intimate.) In addition, just to spice things up a little more, there is a kinky BDS&M current running not so far under the surface of these films.

In the erotic thriller, sex is dangerous, and often fatal. Therefore, the '40s *femme fatale* made a comeback with Stone and Barkin, along with her aerodynamic shoulder pads and leather jackets. This time the character took the form of the aggressive single woman, who tomcatted around like a man. But, this roving woman soon got her own comeuppance in films like *Single White Female* and *Looking for Mr. Goodbar.*

The thrill was quickly gone with this sexually adventurous character. The movies that featured her soon became ripe for parody and the genre mostly disappeared.

However, audiences are now occasionally willing to forgive this killer-in-lipstick if the sex is of the lesbian variety, as in Atom Egoyan's *Chloe*. Increasingly, gay sex between women is portrayed in a favorable light. Despite the novelty of a couple of gay cowboys getting their freak on in *Brokeback Mountain*, that movie does not seem to have triggered any avalanche of gay-friendly films. Furthermore, May-December sex is increasingly seen to be in the "monstrous" category – Woody Allen and 17-year old Mariel Hemingway in *Manhattan*, notwithstanding.

THE OCCASIONAL FILM DEALING with sexuality stands outside category. David Cronenberg's *A History of Violence* is not exactly an erotic thriller. In the film, there is violent sex between Viggo Mortenson and Maria Bello, but they are reflective of the strains in their marriage caused by the revelation that he is, in fact, Joey, a hit man for the Outfit. The scene is remarkable in the way it combines sex, emotion, and violence all in one. Slaps lead to lovemaking on a stairwell, as anger and lust combine and panties get ripped and passion is unleashed.

In a time when raw pornography is readily available, the writer must present the viewers with something different if he wishes to capture their attention. Nowadays, the plain old missionary position just won't do. Nor will the entire Kama Sutra of positions and combinations. You don't have to visit a movie theatre to see any kink that suits. Pornography leaves one wondering about the lives of those men and women humping so furiously away. The attempts to actually portray character in these sordid little playlets, not to mention the acting and direction, are so risible that we'll never know.

All the same, there's something to be learned from pornography, just as there is from street graffiti. Both express powerful instincts that the aspiring writer would do well to harness for his own depictions of sex.

(Actually, as the writer of the cable movie, *Rated X,* starring the great Charlie Sheen, the story of the notorious Mitchell Brothers of San Francisco, I do know something about the off-screen lives of porn stars. I happen to have interviewed a number of them. A sadder, more prosaic lot of humans it has never been my misfortune to encounter.)

In any event, audiences have seen so many sex scenes over the years that tedium has set in.

Still, a writer must be audacious, even in a society where family values and pornography uneasily co-exist. This is done, I believe, by concentrating on the characters and their relationships, as extended into their sexuality.

In any event, it's just as interesting to me to see how people end up in bed as to witness what they do when they get there. Unfortunately, we seldom learn from a film how it happens; seduction, mutual or otherwise, is generally left to the imagination. Boy and girl smile winsomely at each other, and then we cut to them pumping furiously away.

Good old Vinny Lawrence, back in the '30s, had some instructive thoughts on this matter. He found the conventional way of depicting gathering romance, walks on the beach, listening to music together, etc. unconvincing. He suggested to James M. Cain that the fatal moment could be better depicted if one of the partners was resisting sexual involvement.

In Lawrence's version, the guy resists because he thinks the girl too young. Then, friends, they go fishing. In wifely fashion, she offers to cook the trout he's caught, and *bingo* – around her go his arms.

For a couple of decades, explicit sexual scenes were almost obligatory. Now, matters have returned to the embrace, followed by the post-coital discussion pattern of earlier times.

Generally, sex has been portrayed in movies in a positive light. Sex was generally accounted a good thing. But now, films like *The Girl with the Dragon Tattoo,* with its prolonged depictions of anal rape, and *Shame,* with its portrayal of sex as addiction, as the critic Bart Testa has observed, may be sending films in the opposite direction. Now, depicting sex as dysfunction may be the Puritanism of the cinema's future.

WRITING FUNNY

IT'S IMPOSSIBLE TO TEACH A WRITER to be funny. You either wake up in the morning with a sense of humor or you don't. Bruce Jay Friedman, one of America's best comic writers, maintains that the key to writing comedy is to be out of control but presentable at meetings. Fundamentally, if your protagonist is a funny character, you have a funny story. I didn't start out to write *Casino Jack* as a comedy. But, in real life, Jack Abramoff was a quipster. So I gave him a bunch of quips. The result was black comedy.

Audiences always need to laugh. No matter the vagaries of film and television, that truth never changes. Basically, if you can write funny, you will never be out of a job. Fortunately, the archetypal characters of comedy, stretching back to Greek drama, are infinitely recyclable. The dumb blonde, the nerd, the absent-minded professor, the dim-witted jock, the miser, the slacker, the zealot, are always available for the writer to exploit, since the audience never tires of them.

The trick here is in the character relationships. Put your comic protagonist up against his dramatic opposite. Give the miser a spendthrift wife or have the high school nerd fall in love with a sexy cheerleader; with a little luck, laughs are the result.

For example, the dumb blonde archetype has been up-dated fairly recently with Reese Witherspoon in *Legally Blonde*. In this film, Witherspoon plays a plucky sorority queen, a fish out of water at Harvard Law, trying to get her snooty law student boyfriend back after he's dumped her. Using her girly-girly ways, Reese helps the obligatory tough Harvard law prof win a murder case and finds true love too.

Audiences find weakness perennially funny. Shallowness, stupidity, cheapness, selfishness, social awkwardness, are all bountiful sources of humour. After all, ridicule is a substitute for assault. Therefore, comedians are notoriously aggressive people. Fortunately for the writer, human weakness is plentiful; it's something we're all provided with. It's just that, like everything else, these foibles, as comedy fodder, change with the times.

For instance, audiences from time immemorial found drunks funny. Red Skelton or Jackie Gleason would stagger and slobber around and the entire theater would fall on the floor, busting a gut.

No longer.

Now, alcoholism is a "serious disease" and must be taken with a straight face. Instead, fortunately, we have stoner humour. All a writer has to do is set out a marijuana bong onscreen and audiences start to giggle. Wine or weed, human weakness of one sort or another, is on display for our amusement.

In the Coen Brothers' cult film, *The Big Lebowski,* a parody of *The Big Sleep,* most of the humour comes out of the character of the stoner hero, the Dude, Jeff Lebowski. Played by Jeff Bridges, the Dude, is a former '60s radical and definitely "the laziest man in L.A. County."

Freud said that wit consists of displacement. So, Lebowski, the unemployed slacker, carries himself like a Lord of Creation, affecting the exquisite taste of an interior decorator. When comic German nihilist thugs steal a rug from his apartment, the Dude says, "That rug really held the room together." Of course, the room is a shithole; that's what's so funny. The thugs are looking for another Lebowski's wife, in a bit of mistaken identity. Quips the Dude: "Does this place look like I'm fucking married? All my plants are dead."

The Dude, an enthusiastic bowler, is also described as "a rumpled man in whom casualness runs deep." Against the Dude's relaxed air, the Coens counterpoint a range of loser characters in terminal states of contemporary rage. Accordingly, the other major source of humour in *The Big Lebowski* is Walter Sobchuk, an angry Vietnam vet, played by John Goodman. Like '60s political radical Lebowski, Vietnam vet is a figure from the past, a fish out of water in the Republican present.

Next to the Father of the Shortstop, the Vietnam vet has to be the stalest character in cinema, but the Coen Brothers make him work, one more time, because anger is funny. They also make Walter a convert to Orthodox Judaism so he is prone to saying things like, "I told that Kraut a fucking thousand times I don't roll *on Shabbos!*" The Dude and Walter, grown men wearing Bermuda shorts, may be the funniest comic duo since Abbott and Costello or Martin and Lewis.

Another man with the same name, the millionaire, Jeffrey Lebowski, plays General Sternwood to the Dude's slacker Marlowe. The Big Lebowski of the title, a Reaganite free-enterpriser, is in a comic state of rage against "bums." Jesus Quintana, the Dude's rival in bowling, and a convicted pedophile, is also in a homicidal rage whose origins remain mysterious. When Jesus rants at the Dude and Walter, threatening to stick a pistol up Walter's butt and pull the trigger till it goes "click," Walter counters with a simple, heartfelt, "Jesus!" Responds Quintana, "Nobody fucks with the Jesus."

In *The Producers*, Bloom is passive, timid, and repressed. Bialystock is flamboyant, outrageous, devious, and corrupt, the classic Jewish *hondler.* The collision of these personalities, in the context of the '50s Broadway milieu, creates the humour.

Psychological displacement is also used in comedy when characters act incongruously. The Santa Claus who's a misanthrope and hates everybody, as in *Bad Santa,* the schoolteacher who's utterly selfish and cares nothing for her students, as in *Bad Teacher*, blues musicians who act and dress like '50s TV detectives, as in *The Blues Brothers*.

In addition to comic characters like Bad Santa and the Blues Brothers, archetypal situations are perennially funny. The TV sitcom could not exist without the mother-in-law visit, since close proximity naturally creates comic drama. For similar reasons, offices are constant sources of sitcom fodder. Intrusion, as well, is a reliable source of dramatic humour: people showing up at the wrong time and place. *The Cable Guy*, for instance, merely consists of Jim Carrey turning up at Matthew Broderick's apartment at precisely the wrong time... *just wanting to be his friend.*

As editorial cartoonists are well aware, anybody can be satirized, especially if they're figures in public life. Despite the famous Broadway encomium that satire closes after a week, scorching comedy such as Stanley Kubrick and Terry Southern's *Dr. Strangelove or: How I Learned to Stop Worrying and Love the Bomb*, must serve as any writer's model for anyone who aspires to write black humour. It's hard to be more audacious than a comedy about nuclear war.

Terry Southern, that most underrated of American novelists, created his outrageous characters by taking them directly from the headlines of the time – the late '50s and early '60s, when the world was marooned in the depths of the Cold War.

Brigadier General Jack D. Ripper, General "Buck" Turgidson, Colonel "Bat" Guano, Major T.J. "King" Kong, are all only slight exaggerations of the personalities of the Cold War militarists of the time. Anticipating the Coen Brothers' dramatic strategy by a few decades, Southern created a foil for their rage in gentle President Merkin Muffley, a passive, Adlai Stevenson-like chief executive. When a missile attack on the Soviet Union is deliberately launched by the maniacal General Ripper in crankish protest against the fluoridation of the water supply, President Muffley must save the world from nuclear Armageddon.

The most memorable of the multiple characters Peter Sellers portrays is Dr. Strangelove, the wheelchair-bound missile expert and former Nazi who has trouble controlling his arm, which is always trying to deliver a Hitler salute. As Major Kong, played by Stetson-wearing Slim Pickens, rides the fatal rocket down into Russia like a bucking bronco, Dr Strangelove screams, "*Mein Fuehrer, I can walk!*"

Although Strangelove is based on Dr. Werner von Braun, Terry Southern's comic character looks forward to all those bloodthirsty wheelchair pundits, mostly of East European origin, who never met a foreign war they didn't like, just so long as somebody else fought it. Although current events are always fodder for television skit humour, it's rare to find a full-length drama as perfectly structured as Southern and Kubrick's. The film is loosely based on a Cold War thriller, *Red Alert*, which featured a nuclear disaster scenario, but done with a straight face. In large part, the brilliance of *Strangelove* is due to Southern's unsurpassed willingness to push the caricature as far as he does, and Kubrick's ability, not to mention his command of resources, to put it on the screen. To this point, no writer or director has succeeded half so well. What is perhaps missing from any such satires is the intensity of loathing behind Southern's political caricatures. Few personalities inspire the sort of revulsion as much as those corn-pone sorts who would have blown up the planet on behalf of one ideology or another.

TROPIC THUNDER IS OSTENSIBLY an update on military satire, a send-up of blood-and-guts combat films with their gore and self-sacrificing heroism. In reality, the movie spoofs filmmaking itself, with an insider's knowledge. The film's protagonist, Tugg Speedman, is a fading action hero à la Sly Stallone. Kirk

Lazarus is a five-time Oscar-winning Australian method actor à la Russell Crowe. Jeff Portnoy is a drug-addicted comedian who has made his reputation with fart jokes. Damien Cockburn is a rookie director who can't control his actors and is a month behind schedule. Les Grossman is a brutal, overbearing studio head. John "Four Leaf" Tayback is a crusty, hook-handed Vietnam vet, whose memoir is being made into a film in the jungle.

The most knowing of the inside jokes in the film are the ones that recount Tugg Speedman's failed attempts to restore lost prominence with a series of pandering roles, including "Simple Jack," a mentally impaired farm boy who can "talk" to animals, an eerily prescient version of Albert, the dim farm lad in *War Horse*. Hilariously, Lazarus tells Speedman, "Everybody knows you never go full retard."

Solid professional advice, for writers as well as actors.

Never go the full retard.

Even in a comedy.

COMEDY, LIKE VIOLENT ACTION, is a function of national culture. American comedy, especially television comedy, has to have two or three loud yucks on every page. British comedy, naturally, is drier, without all the gags. British viewers are unfailingly amused, as in *The Office,* by the sight of a foolish character acting foolishly, usually in the grip of some mania or self-deception.

As a Canadian writer, I'm somewhere in between. Both the protagonists of *Dead Ringers* and *Casino Jack* are virtuosos of self-deception, but I like to occasionally give them lines of comic dialogue.

Comedic dialogue, in its structure, is identical to the jokes of vaudeville and music hall: set up and punch line. For instance, in *Tropic Thunder*, Tugg Speedman who has just murdered a panda, is talking with his agent, Rick. He tells him that he just killed the thing he loves most in the world. "Oh, Jesus," says Rick, "You killed a hooker."

Scatology, like so much else in drama, goes back to the Greeks. Recently, toilet humour is making a major comeback, as films aim at a younger and dumber audience.

Flatulence, masturbation, incontinence, projectile vomiting and all the rest have become the everyday staples of comedy. Producers are increasingly prone to suggesting to writers that they, you know, write a scene where the hero pisses the bed. But, when it comes to writing caca and fart jokes, in the words of Sam Goldwyn, "Include me out." More than anything else, scatology represents the infantilization of the cinema.

ADAPTATION
AND COLLABORATION

FILM MAKES USE OF EVERY conceivable media as raw material.

Many of the films discussed to this point have been adapted from novels. It could be said, with a certain degree of accuracy, that other media often represent the content of movies. Adapting the novel, or any other book, stage play, newspaper or magazine article, TV shows, foreign films, graphic novels, or comic book, remains a substantial part of the art of screenwriting. Adaptation, naturally, is an oft-maligned process, especially by the writers whose books or plays have been mangled by the movies.

Of course, many novels are not readily adapted to film. A successful narrative does not necessarily make a successful drama. Lightly plotted character studies, or, stream-of-consciousness fiction devoted to the character's inner life are not really suited to film. Saul Bellow's Mr. Sammler, peering in the mirror, ruminating how the world has gone to hell in a handbasket, is not really a movie character. So, too, the novels of Robertson Davies, even with his fusty 19th-century theatrical aura: they are not susceptible to dramatization; many have tried and many have failed. Unfortunately, most literary novels rely on lyric eloquence; the writer's narrative voice is what's important. Voice alone doesn't cut it in a visual medium.

There are no hard and fast rules for turning a book into a movie. John Huston, famously, had a secretary type up *The Maltese Falcon* in screenplay form and shot the typescript. *There Will Be Blood,* Paul Thomas Anderson's adaptation of Upton Sinclair's novel, *Oil!,* is made up of only a few chapters of the original. Alvin Sargent adapted *Julia* from a single chapter of Lillian Hellman's memoir, *Pentimento.*

Sargent, the definitive Hollywood screenwriter, won the Academy Award for his screenplay; then won it again a few years late for *Ordinary People.* A couple decades later, Sargent co-wrote *Spider-Man 3,* presumably overjoyed to get the studio assignment.

Roll with the punches, baby.

The trick in adaptation is to conceptualize a movie that could be made from the materials of the book. This concept is your "take." You should be able to see, in your mind's eye, before committing a word to paper, the movie you want to make from the first shot right to the end titles. The writer then must apply the dramatic conventions we have been discussing and put them to work on the book. If the result is faithful to the original, so much the better.

If not, too bad.

Better to violate the book and write a strong script than be faithful to it and turn one in that fails. If your movie is true to the novel, that's a bonus.

The list of great books that have made lousy movies is a long one. *Catch-22, The Great Gatsby, The Naked and the Dead, Moby Dick, Ulysses, Ragtime, A Walk on the Wild Side, The Bonfire of the Vanities* – well, one could go on.

On the other side of the ledger are a few classic novels that have succeeded as films, among them, *A Passage to India, From Here to Eternity, Ironweed, Revolutionary Road, Heart of Darkness,* and *Of Human Bondage.*

As mentioned previously, there are certain classic novelists whose work is inherently dramatic and most of whose novels have been filmed: Austen, James, Graham Greene, and Dickens.

Greene's *The Third Man* is one of the few examples of a great movie written by a writer who was also a great novelist. Fitzgerald was a famous failure in the movies. Faulkner, with the exception of *The Big Sleep,* toiled anonymously, as did Nathaniel West, James M. Cain, Brian Moore, William Kennedy, and many others.

The popular elements that make good movies – suspense, violence, and nudity, often, in themselves, are regarded as *déclassé* in the quality lit biz: accordingly, genre novels, from detective stories to horror and science fiction, offer the best raw material for films. The studios will always buy the rights to bestselling novels since they have a ready-made audience and name recognition. A star actor in a popular book ought to be a surefire recipe for success. Except – it often isn't.

However, the beginning screenwriter can do worse than adapting a novel first time out. For one thing, characters and plot come ready-made, and the rights to a modestly successful recent novel, or an underrated one by a lesser-known writer, come fairly cheap. (Of course, the novelist may not want to sell the rights at all or prefer to hang out for that big-time offer he believes must eventually come. If so, move on to the next book; there's lots of them available.)

However, when it comes to adapting a book, the screenwriter should know it just as well as the guy who wrote it. Reading the material five times is just the beginning. You should mark the passages you believe must be in the film each time through. If these passages end up with a mark beside them every time, there's no way they can be kept out of a film.

There are many creative strategies to be considered in adapting a novel. Updating the story is just one. Joseph Conrad's *Heart of Darkness* was moved from the Belgian Congo in the 19th century to the American war in Vietnam in *Apocalypse Now*. Nathaniel Hawthorne's *The Scarlet Letter* was taken out of Puritan New England and turned into a contemporary teen drama in *Easy A*. Richard Price and Martin Scorsese transformed the tortured Russian of *The Gambler* into a bearish American Abstract Expressionist played by Nick Nolte in their episode, "Life Lessons," in *New York Stories*.

New technologies represent opportunities to rescue material from the far past. Using super-imposition chroma key in *300*, Zack Snyder retold the Battle of Thermopylae, via Frank Miller's comic book. The story of outnumbered ancient Greeks in hand-to-hand combat against Xerxes and his Persian armies found a receptive audience in the days after 9/11.

It, nonetheless, took an admirable leap of the imagination to bring back that discarded genre of the '50s, the Classical Epic, in new cinematic guise. A combat sequence with archers, spears and hand-to-hand fighting with swords, takes on a completely new aura in the age of CGI-driven action sequences. It seems to matter little in the world-creation genre whether it's the imaginary future or the ancient past, just so long as the viewer is transported to a world sufficiently different from this one. It's no secret that science fiction and fantasy writers routinely pillage obscure corners of history for their material, confident that untutored readers will never be any the wiser.

Magazine articles also represent a fertile source of material for the movies – the best example being *Saturday Night Fever,* adapted from an article that originally appeared in *New York* magazine. That the article turned out to be largely fiction, made up out of whole cloth by the "journalist," did not detract from the movie a bit. Another movie based on a magazine article, *Adaptation,* turned out to be a film about the travails encountered by the screenwriter Charlie Kaufman in adapting a piece from *The New Yorker.*

(In Hollywood, every aspect of screenwriting is turned into a specialty by somebody or other. There are comedy gag writers, writers who specialize in thinking up action gags. And there are researchers whose job it is to comb newspapers and magazines looking for story material.)

Hollywood loves to adapt foreign films and television – with mixed results. I was once hired to turn a famous British crime miniseries into a feature film. It wasn't so difficult to boil down the six hours into 90 minutes. It was just that all the charm of the piece resided in the Britishness of the characters: the charismatic East End villain, the poor bloke cop. Transformed into Americans, they became flat, prosaic, ordinary.

AS FAR AS COLLABORATION with another writer goes, the best adage to remember is Cindy Lauper's – *money changes everything*. You might be best friends with another writer at the beginning of collaboration; you may well not be before it's over.

It's also important to remember, before committing yourself to a writing partnership, even for one project, that your partner's reputation becomes yours, for better or worse.

There's a famous Hollywood story about a writing team, one of whom became involved with a woman producer. When the lady in question was got with child, the guy went down to the corner for cigarettes, never to return. Out on the woman producer jungle drums went the word – these writers will never work again. The careless seducer's innocent partner never knew what hit him.

But his screenwriting career was over.

In the age of gender equality, the casting couch cuts both ways. Woman producers are not proof against masculine attraction. And looks and charm can indeed help in landing a screenwriting assignment. Story conferences are more pleasant at lunches and dinners. Research trips to exotic locales are often necessary. Quite possibly, that fatal moment we discussed earlier arrives right on cue. The prudent writer will suddenly develop an urgent appointment elsewhere since the odds of the romance turning into trouble are fairly high. But then, screenwriting is no occupation for the prudent in the first place... Well, they say mistakes are merely the portals of discovery...

Leaving romance aside for the moment, there are various levels of collaboration in the movies. In the breaking into the business stage, two buddies – of either sex – team up to write a script. There they are. They have a wonderful friendship. They've talked endlessly about film over drinks or lunch. They go to the movies together. It seems a lot better to work together than suffer alone in a room.

First, they have to decide who's going to put the actual words down on paper, and who's going to just, you know, sit there across the desk and... *spitball.*

Soon they find the guy who does the actual typing has all the power. After all the palavering and arguments, he can refuse to insert the other writer's ideas into the script. Or, they find that one of the team is doing all the actual work. Or, they find that one of the collaborators has some very curious notions about what a movie is all about. One partner develops some strong reservations about those snakes and reptiles he secretly finds lurking in the recesses of the other's psyche, vicious creatures that he never suspected over lunch. They're both looking at the same animal; it's just that one of them thinks it's blue; the other thinks it's violent, screaming-bloody scarlet.

The novelist Nelson Algren's first rule of life was to never sleep with a woman with more troubles than he had. The screenwriting corollary is that you should never collaborate with a writer with less talent than yourself.

Despite all of this, there are some successful writing teams. *Somewhere.*

I, personally, prefer to suffer alone.

Less permanent arrangements for collaboration than the writing team are routine in films. Most producers, directors, and lead actors have the contractual right to give a writer "notes." Notes take the form of laundry lists of objections, going from the cosmic and grandiose to the breathtakingly petty.

Many odd sorts of people fancy themselves as producers, some of them with a shaky grasp on literacy. Movies, with all their glamour, attract a lot of sketchy characters. Still, they all know what they, or their girlfriends, like.

Responding to notes takes all the devious ingenuity of the trapped rodent. You can say straight out what you think of the notes: it's best to have another project lined up, if you're going to do so. You can't defend what you've done; it's considered obstructive. Besides, they all outrank you. What you need to do is come to the story conference armed with a ton of ideas for the rewrite and ready to out-talk anybody.

These story conferences have a dynamic of their own. It's often the case that a movie appears with a first-rate cast, director, written by somebody who's done strong work in the past – and stinks out the joint. What has usually happened is that writer(s) and director have, at the end of endless drafts, agreed on a compromise that settles their differences but makes little actual dramatic sense. They are writing in circles, doing revision after revision, possibly going past a draft that works in favor of one that doesn't. After about 10 or 15 passes at the material, nobody knows which way is up. Often, the collective reputations of everybody involved are sufficient to get the movie made. The critics have a field day with the results.

The professional circumstances under which collaboration is undertaken often determine its outcome. If a director is hired onto a project whose script has been written, he will often seek to dislodge the original writer and bring on somebody he has worked with in the past. If you happen to be the original writer, you'll discover ridiculous requests being deliberately made. Give the guy what he wants; he's just laying traps so you can have a vicious disagreement and he can go to the producers and say, "I can't work with this nitwit."

In a week or so, he'll forget all about the intentionally dumb requests and you can take them out.

Conversely, if you have been hired to rewrite a director's script, he is likely not to regard you in a friendly light either. It is the conceit of many directors that they are also writers. Certainly, some of them are. All too often the writer is on the lookout for a devious method of ridding the script of clunky dialogue, plot improbabilities and all the rest. All his persuasive and diplomatic resources are necessarily on call.

Ultimately, a good director or producer knows how to work with writers and knows how to get their best out of them. Unfortunately, you never know how collaboration will work until you're in the middle of it. Of course, the vagaries of the business are such that you are often thrown in with collaborators who prove unsympathetic.

Once, I found myself in collaboration with a well-known director. The gig: turn the plot of the opera, *Pagliacci*, into a modern-day drama. The plot, where a jealous circus clown tragically murders his lover, was just my sort of thing. I found this down-at-the-heels circus in the outskirts of Montreal that would have made Fellini leap with joy. Love triangles are to me what lilies are to Monet: a perennial source of inspiration. Wrote up the script and handed it in only to be met by silence, the sort of silence that can only mean one thing. (Generally, if a collaborator likes your work, he can't wait to get on a phone to tell you.) The director didn't want a funky little circus; he wanted a spiffy Cirque du Soleil operation. He didn't want a tragic triangle leading to murder; he wanted the clown to *save* his lover from the depredations of the other man.

Onto the next hack.

Another famous director received me at a first-story conference in his office in fashionable Santa Monica while getting a haircut. The message was clear: in the scheme of my life, you, as a writer rank about equal to my hair stylist. This inauspicious beginning set the tone for the collaboration as a whole.

A not-so-famous director informed me, just as we were about go into production with a crime thriller I had written, that Quentin Tarantino was a force for evil in the universe.

I knew my film was doomed.

Not all tales of collaboration end badly. There are directors and actors, thank God, whose suggestions actually improve your work, whose instincts can generally be trusted to be in harmony with your own. The best thing to do is arrange to work with them whenever practical.

The reality is, that the screenwriter has very little to do with who ultimately directs his script. The secret to making certain your script is not ruined is to make it director-proof, a feat that takes some very strong writing indeed.

The director-proof script is one that so transparently works that it is obvious to everybody concerned that to tamper with it by so much as a comma would represent a travesty. There are not many scripts like that around, and not that many producers who would recognize one.

But, you can always hope.

Rewrites are a form of involuntary collaboration. Down in the trenches of the movie business, screenwriters are rewriting others and being rewritten themselves. When they've lost patience with a writer, a fairly frequent occurrence, producers take pitches on the rewrite. When you go in to deliver your take, there's always an assistant present, taking notes. There's always a chance they'll purloin your take and hand it to a pet writer. ("Hey, how about handling it this way.")

Nothing much you can do about it.

Writers start out sincere and good-hearted, wanting to keep a brother writer's best work intact, etc etc. After a few bad experiences on the other end of a rewrite, they're ready to jettison the other guy's work holus-bolus, whether it works or not, in order to get that all-important lead credit.

If you're a staff writer, on a television show, say, your job is to rewrite the drafts of others to the specifications of the show and to make adjustments to production budget realities. If you reduce the number of scenes, you reduce the number of lighting set-ups. If you reduce the number of exteriors, there are fewer expensive locations to film.

That sort of thing.

I once did some time as a staff writer in television. It was a co-production with Canada, the U.S., Germany, and France. The Canadians thought it was a sci-fi show, the Americans thought it was a crime show, the Germans thought it was a sex show and the French thought it was a kids show. I was making around $6,000 a week.

Fun and games.

I quit shortly after a story conference where I was talking about *The Blue Angel,* the classic German film starring Marlene Dietrich, and the show's exec producer thought I meant the U.S. air force's stunt flying team.

KILLING IN THE
ROOM: THE INDUSTRY
AND YOU

I REMEMBER ONCE GOING to a meeting at Jody Foster's office in Los Angeles. Even for Hollywood, the security arrangements were intimidating and bunker-like, an elaborate series of locked doors. The intercoms, buzzing with electronic distortion, blared interrogation from Foster's staff to visitors. I was taken aback until I remembered that the actress had been subject to the attentions of John Hinckley, Jr., the guy who had tried to take Reagan out.

He was a big fan of her work in *Taxi Driver.*

It's not news that there's something about the movies that promotes mass hysteria. I believe Nathanael West had a few words to say on that subject back in the '30s in *The Day of the Locust.* In any event, there's a huge, violent pressure on people like Foster with the ability to make movies happen. Unless you have access to the proper channels, they're impossible to get to. I know entire countries that are easier to enter at border points than studio lots, if you don't happen to have the proper authorization. The security's that heavy.

For some odd reason, there is nobody on the planet who doesn't assume they have a future in showbiz, if they only tried. When students take a course in screenwriting, their most insistent question is, "How do I break in?"

If everybody could, everybody would.

So, the answer is, "Write something good."

A strong script is a battering ram that can break down all those barriers between you and the people who can make it happen.

Now, it's pretty safe to say that there are very few unproduced masterpieces lying around. Of course, there are always good scripts that for one reason or another miss the mark. But, even if the aspiring writer manages to complete a script that truly qualifies as a masterpiece, there are plenty of talent agents around who would sign them up on the chance that they could write another such script.

(An agent friend once told me of a writer who produced 17 unproduced scripts in a row and retired with a Writers Guild pension of $100,000 a year. Believe me, writers with that kind of talent are thin on the ground.)

The movies are an art form of incomparable beauty; they are also a tough racket. If it's hard to break into the business, it's also hard to stay in it.

So, the best answer is, if you write a script that clearly deserves to be made, good things will happen. Movies are magic, but the first place that magic resides is inside you. It's unobtainable, otherwise.

At any rate, I'm reminded of a story told by a screenwriting friend. Years ago, as a young man, he was in New York, waiting tables, the perennial occupation of showbiz wannabes. One of the restaurant's customers was Francis Ford Coppola. My buddy asked Coppola how to break into movies.

The great man said, "Do you have a relative in the business?"

That's still the best way.

Failing that, there are some well-trodden paths for screenwriters, generally available to people in their 20s, starting out in life.

Film school, an internship on a television series, writing for television, then moving on to features. That's a typical screenwriting career. The prime requisite for that path, however, is a sort of bland proficiency. It's the writing equivalent of being a studio musician; the sort of cat who can play anything that's put in front of him. There's a lot of financial satisfaction in that sort of career, not so much of the creative sort.

(The fundamental thrill in screenwriting is to see the images and voices that have originated solely in your head up there on a giant screen in a full theatre.)

Or, another career strategy: move to Los Angeles, day gig answering phones, writing at night, and hope that the screenplay gets picked up. Of course, every waiter, every grip, every assistant is famously working on a screenplay. That doesn't mean that, every once in a while, one of them sells one. But then, people win the lottery too.

For those who come late to the game, it has to be said there is no formula.

"My Way" is not just Frank Sinatra's mantra. It applies to everybody.

There are as many paths to screenwriting careers as there are people. Just as important as going out and selling yourself is establishing an identity, as the commercial jargon of our time has it, a "brand." You need to discover an affinity for a genre, a style, and stick to it.

Screenwriters, like actors, are typecast. For five years after *Dead Ringers,* I was the writing equivalent of Peter Lorre. Every weird, horrific project around, once I got Hollywood representation, came my way. Not that I was complaining. If I wanted to be known for something else, it was up to me to prove I could do it.

Films and television are global now; there are many different milieus, many niches. Women's networks, sci-fi networks, producers who specialize in dramas of every stripe. Before the aspiring writer pursues an idea, he should ask himself who he might sell it to, what niche could it fill.

Film students, typically, believe that writing low-budget horror is a tried and true way into the business. After all, it's worked many times before. The problem is the world is full of thousands of low-budget horror scripts written by film school graduates, one very similar to the other.

It must be said, though, that unless you have more than a hint of the Sammy Glick hustler in your soul, the film business is not for you.

As Vinny Lawrence would put it, it's a business of relationships.

To tell the truth, I'm uncertain as to how to suggest forming relationships; it's like giving dating advice. How does anybody get together in an artistic venture? A guy with a guitar on a bus meets another guy on the bus; they start talking about music; the rest is history.

Besides meeting David Cronenberg in college, my introduction to the movies happened this way. It was the early '70s. I was living in what, in retrospect, would be called a hippie house on Avenue Road in Toronto. All we did was sit around, smoke dope, watch movies and talk about them. Living in the house was a nifty Australian blonde named Diane who I had met on the Greek isle of Hydra. We had one of those equivocal friendships that every so often threatened to become romantic but never actually did. She showed up one night with a well-known film director. (It must be said; Diane was just a little bit of a groupie.) The director and I got talking about movies. I showed him an outline for a film I had written. He liked it and suggested we work on the script together. I learned a lot. A couple of years later, the movie appeared. Once I had a look at what happened to my script I decided that movies were not my thing. I swore off them. I was 26. A few years later, I reconsidered my position.

All those years ago, it was much easier to break in. It wasn't hard to get to see people. Jobs in the business were there, seemingly for the asking. There were no film schools pumping out graduates, all competing with one another for the same spots.

In those days, sitting alone in a room was difficult for me. There was a big bright world out there. Going into a room and talking some guy's brains out was a lot easier than writing. I enjoyed the challenge; it was fun.

Movies are not the great American art form. The pitch meeting is the great American art form, not just in showbiz, but also in the business world. Although writing requires extended periods of sitting in front of a computer alone, mining those inner depths, getting the screenplay out into the world requires the attitude of a salesman in a haberdashery. The customer who comes in unwilling to buy must be sold two suits, five shirts, and a pair of shoes.

The arena in which the pitch meeting takes place is known as "the room." It is to the movies what the ring is to boxing, what the ice is to hockey – the room is where lives and careers are won and lost. Sometimes the room is a boardroom, other times it's just somebody's office. The two opposing teams are the people who are buying and the people who are selling.

You're with the sellers.

There is a type of filmmaker who has mastered the pitch meeting; he's the emperor of the room. This guy reads the trades everyday like a racetrack tout reads the *Racing Form*. He confabulates a grand cosmic scheme about where the biz is going in general. He studies what films or TV dramas the network or production company has made in the past year. He checks how they made out with the critics, what kind of audience they drew.

In the room he's almost tap dancing as he lays down to the assembled Suits just how what he has to sell fits their company's needs exactly, not too mention how it fits perfectly into the grand media design of the universe. He gets so carried away with excitement that he just about jumps up on the desk or boardroom table. The greatest outcome of any pitch meeting is that the Suits "buy it in the room."

Just stop by Business Affairs and pick up the cheque.

There's a certain kind of writer, or producer, with a gift for the gab, the kind of gent, who, as they say, can sell ice cream to the Eskimos, or Inuit, as I must now say. Usually, this guy's problems come later, when he actually has to write the idea he's sold. This glib fellow is also an expert in the art of reading faces and reactions, so he doesn't go in with a fixed pitch; he alters the story and characters as he goes along, making sure the buyers are with him. He's made the sale but he can't quite remember just what it was he put across.

Of course, nobody in Hollywood actually says "No." That's too unpleasant. I picked up an agent after *Dead Ringers* and he sent me on the Hollywood rounds. I came up with a few story ideas and bravely set forth pitching them to potential buyers. In one office, the people gathered round and reacted to my pitch with chuckles and appreciation. They called in the secretaries and assistants to hear it, they liked it so much. They all thought my story was wonderful.

Jesus, I thought, *I am truly a genius. First time out in Hollywood and I've sold a goddamn picture.*

Of course, I never heard from anybody, ever again.

Radio silence is the conventional method of communicating disapproval in Hollywood. Nobody wants to have an unpleasant conversation.

Often, you never really know the reason something is dropped. As a writer, you are way down the food chain. The decisions, yea or nay, vis-à-vis production get made at the very top of the food chain of the giant companies like Time Warner that own the studios and networks. It often has nothing to do with the quality of your work, but with the various strategic and corporate factors that you have no way of anticipating.

The green light must flash at every level of the corporate structure, and it can suddenly stall and die at any level. Each executive decision takes at least a week to make. Hanging on the phone will only drive you crazy; bugging everybody involved for news will only increase your rep as a neurotic. This is the stage where it's useful to have a hobby or serious vice to cultivate.

Occasionally, the absurdity of the biz works in your favor. Once, I had a development deal with a certain star husband-and-wife team. Shortly after the deal was signed, the lovers went what the Rat Pack used to call Splitsville. Their company was contractually obliged to pay me the full shot, a tidy sum. I hadn't written Word One.

When it's working for you, Hollywood is a wonderful town.

Once your script has the green light, they don't really need you any more. If you've maintained a good relationship with the producers and directors, they'll keep you involved on the fringes. If they don't enjoy your company, and the battles over the script have been particularly nasty, it's like, *See you at the premiere, dude.*

Keeping and maintaining the commitment of lead actors is a whole art in itself. Projects with better paydays, or more prestige attached, distract them from yours. Movie stars are easily bored; any delay in attracting financing gives them too much time to think about the role, develop doubts about whether they can play it or not.

Okay. You've sold the outline, written the drafts, and attracted the director and stars. Now, shooting begins.

Depending on how you've been getting on with everybody so far, they may or may not invite you to the set. (Even if the story was your idea and you wrote the first drafts, there might be so many writers between you and the shooting script, nobody wants you around to see your brainstorm get made.)

Strangely enough, there are some drawbacks, mostly of a psychological nature, in seeing a screenplay go into production. It may sound precious to say it, but characters and scenes that have heretofore existed solely in your mind for months, possibly years, become, for you, private property. When all the grips, production secretaries, and day players thumb copies of the script and pass comments on them, those products of your mind seem oddly violated.

On set, there's a definite etiquette. You really shouldn't give the actors notes about their performances unless invited. That's a good way to find yourself disinvited. The writer is occasionally called upon to supply new dialogue or correct old lines. This is where the ability to think on your feet in a room full of people comes in handy.

Otherwise, locations are too much like high school for my liking. Cliques form. People's feelings get hurt because the star didn't invite them golfing or night-clubbing. Who eats lunch with who in whose trailer becomes important. They say that John Huston used to spend downtime playing poker with the grips. Personally, I find the hair and make-up gals and guys to be invariably amusing, in a camp sort of style.

You could do worse.

Once a film is in the can, that's still just the beginning. Editing is a process that remains mysterious to me; we'll skip over it here. Getting distribution for the film is yet another obstacle. Prints and advertising costs can run into the millions.

That's why many films don't see the light of a theatre; no distributor believes he'll recoup the sums he'll lay out. Films that don't receive distribution must be content to play the festival circuit, or be broadcast on cable television.

If you're a director, the festival circuit and promotion tours are the closest you'll ever be to knowing the life of a rock star. The world is full of free drinks and actress wannabes in short skirts. Being the screenwriter is rather like the equivalent of being the bass player.

Who ever heard of the bass player?

Unless you're somebody like David Mamet or Diablo Cody, your name is unlikely to have much marquee value. Publicists tend to shove you in with the supporting cast. I happen to enjoy the company of actors – much more so than that of fellow scribes.

Not to sound sour, though. I think of the kind of moment when the limo is taking you to the premiere of what was once only a glimmer in the corner of your mind. The searchlights are playing across the sky. The fans have gathered outside the theatre – for you and yours. If you can't savor that moment, you never loved the movies in the first place.

FILM STILLS & CREDITS

Introduction
The Big Heat (1953)
Directed by Fritz Lang
Shown: Lee Marvin (as Vince Stone)
Credit: Columbia Pictures/Photofest

Chapter One
Juno (2007)
Directed by Jason Reitman
Shown: Ellen Page
Credit: Fox Searchlight/Photofest

Chapter Two
They Live by Night (1948)
Directed by Nicholas Ray
Shown: Farley Granger, Cathy O'Donnell
Credit: RKO Radio Pictures/Photofest

Chapter Three
White Heat (1949)
Directed by Raoul Walsh
Shown: James Cagney (as Arthur 'Cody' Jarrett)
Credit: Warner Bros. Inc./Photofest

Chapter Four
Dead Ringers (1988)
Directed by David Cronenberg
Shown: Jeremy Irons; center: Geneviève Bujold
Credit: Twentieth Century Fox Film
Corporation/Photofest

Chapter Five
Psycho (1960)
Directed by Alfred Hitchcock
Shown: Janet Leigh
Credit: Paramount Pictures/Photofest

Chapter Six
Pulp Fiction
Directed by Quentin Tarantino
Shown from left: Uma Thurman, John Travolta
Credit: Miramax/Photofest

Chapter Seven
Scarface (1932)
Directed by Howard Hawks
Shown: French Movie Poster / Credit: Photofest

Chapter Eight
Basic Instinct 2 (2006)
Directed by Michael Caton-Jones
Shown: Sharon Stone
Credit: Sony Pictures/Photofest

Chapter Nine
The Big Lebowski (1998)
Directed by Joel Coen
Shown from left: Jeff Bridges (as Jeffrey Lebowski aka
The Dude), John Goodman (as Walter Sobochak)
Credit: Gramercy Pictures/Photofest

Chapter Ten
Of Human Bondage (1934)
Directed by John Cromwell
Shown: Leslie Howard (as Philip Carey),
Bette Davis (as Mildred Rogers)
Credit: RKO/Photofest

Chapter Eleven
The Maltese Falcon (1941)
Directed by John Huston
Shown: Humphrey Bogart (as Sam Spade)
Credit: Warner Bros. Inc./Photofest